Nannie V.

May God al[illegible]
be as real and [illegible]
in your life as [illegible]
has been in mine.

Rhonda
10-5-04

Jet Skiing With God

my wild and victorious ride as a widow!

Psalms 66:16 (NIV) Come and listen, all you who fear God; Let me tell you what he has done for me.

By

Rhonda Clemons

authorHOUSE™
1663 Liberty Drive, Suite 200
Bloomington, Indiana 47403
(800) 839-8640
www.AuthorHouse.com

First published by AuthorHouse 08/13/04

ISBN: 1-4184-0540-X (e)
ISBN: 1-4184-0539-6 (sc)

Printed in the United States of America
Bloomington, Indiana

This book is printed on acid-free paper.

Preface -

I wake up between and 4:00 and 6:00 a.m. just about every day. Sometimes I'm able to go back to sleep but I usually don't. One of my favorite things to do at this early hour is to listen to good praise and worship music and pray. As soon as the sun is up enough, I hit the road for a brisk five-mile walk and my morning quiet time with God. When I walk out of my house in the new morning light, I look up to the sky and say, "Good morning, God" – and then we spend an hour or so in great conversation...

I've been working on this book project for four years now. You see, I was widowed a little over five years ago. About a year after my husband's death, God just laid it on my heart to write about my widow experience. Well, I promptly began putting the thoughts down on paper and immediately I became very depressed. I think when a huge tragedy happens in a person's life, God is gracious and shields our emotions for awhile, making it possible for us to bear up under all that is happening. But at some point a person has to allow those thoughts and feelings to surface and let God walk you through dealing with them. Yet, when I first started dealing with the memories brought about by beginning the book, I just wasn't ready…

Well, in about May 2003, the strong urge to finish the book was once again laid on my heart. God has been so good in the process – I've been able to walk through the memories one more time and although it is painful, I'm filled with a sense of peace about the project. You see, my story is an amazing one and God has shown Himself so powerful in my life each and every day. I think if God could have favorites it would be widows and Fatherless children. In Psalms 146:9 (NIV) it says, "The Lord watches over the alien and sustains the fatherless and the widow, but he frustrates the ways of the wicked." Proverbs 23:10-11 in the NKJV says, "Do not remove the ancient landmark, nor enter the fields of the fatherless; for their Redeemer is mighty; He will plead their case against you." These promises in the Word are very real to me because my family has experienced such protection, provision and blessing since my children and I moved into this category on March 6, 1998

When the book was about 80% complete, I began to think about the title and a verse to don the front cover. Shortly after thinking about this the first time, God brought me to a verse in Psalms for the book cover. Psalms 66:16 (NIV) Come and listen, all you who fear God; let me tell you what he has done for me. When I read that verse the first time I knew without a shadow of a doubt that God had picked out just the perfect one.

I wrestled with the title a little longer though. At first, I was trying to force the issue myself, but I was never at peace about what to call the book. Every couple of days while writing the book in my spare time, I would scrawl a different title on the first page and erase the old thought. It wasn't until this morning that God walked me through a process of thinking about different types of Christian attitudes and how that attitude affects the type of walk you have with God. At the end of the story, was the title...Jet Skiing with God – My Wild and Victorious ride as a Widow.

I know you are thinking – how silly! It struck me that way too at first. But as I thought more about the story that God had painted about attitudes and the resulting level of commitment a person has for God's plan that morning, the title settled very nicely in my thoughts. I then began to visualize the front cover – a very confident mom riding a big jet ski on a magnificent body of water with four beautiful babes in tow! I immediately loved the idea.

I believe there are roughly 3 types of Christian attitudes that result from how willing you are in your heart to participate in God's plan for your life. Depending on how much of your heart you are willing to open up for God, you will in turn be geared a certain way – have an attitude and life that has a very predictable <u>SPEED</u> about it. I see these types of Christians falling in the following speed categories: 1) the golf cart 2) the Camry and 3) the Jet Ski.

A person who lives their Christian life at the golf cart level is willing to open up their heart just enough to receive salvation. This is obviously a good thing! However, a golf cart Christian has only just received enough of God to barely "putt putt" along in this life, slowly inching their way toward heaven. Christians moving along at the golf cart speed in life don't make much of an impact on the world, and for that reason I don't think satan tries to mess in their business in a huge and mighty way – why should he, they aren't causing him and his team much damage?

Now a Christian at the Camry level has also received salvation but they have given God a larger share of their heart. They are willing to stretch some, allow circumstances in life to build their faith and in turn, they are cruising along at a faster clip. Living the Christian life at the Camry speed can be fulfilling because it's not too dangerous. Life at this speed is pleasant, pretty predictable, and it doesn't cause your heart to land in your throat or wonder much what is next. Satan will be after a Camry Christian to a certain degree. He will, in his own boring and predictable way, throw a few nails along the highway, cut a hose once in awhile, blow a head gasket – anything to aggravate and frustrate a Camry Christian.

Now a Jet Ski Christian is a much more rare variety. This type of Christian has an ALL or NOTHING mentality about issues that are near and dear to their heart. A person with a Jet Ski heart is like a dog with a bone once they get a hold of God and truly make Him the Lord of their life. A Jet Ski Christian throws open their entire heart to God and makes it evident time and time again that they will be obedient – totally ready to learn, grow, experience, stretch, mature, climb, and achieve all God has planned for them. A Christian with a Jet Ski heart is a thorn in 'ole Satan's side and it is for this reason that the bad guy is gunning for the Jet Ski types. He is cooking up his biggest and best disasters to try to knock down and keep down a Jet Ski Christian. But, true to form, a Jet Ski Christian just holds on tighter to their Lord and Savior and time and time again will rise victorious over the time bombs placed along their path. You see, I understand what makes this type of Christian "tick" because this is exactly where I've been with God the past few years, on a wild and victorious Jet Ski ride with the Lord God Almighty since my husband's death.

Introduction: Life Phases -

For some people I'm sure, their Christian walk goes from 0-60 (my husband was like this). Upon receiving salvation, they have an immediate and intense desire to learn all they can and that desire lasts beyond the initial emotion; they read diligently, pray continually, and they quickly become fully functional, mature Christians serving the Lord and their fellow believers daily. For me, though, the process of becoming a mature believer has taken a longer route. When I look back on my life, I can see four very distinct stages that my Christian walk has evolved through:

Phase 1) The Head Knowledge Phase

Phase 2) The Shirt-tail Phase

Phase 3) Widowed or rules, rules, and more rules

Phase 4) Freedom or falling in love with Jesus Phase

Let's explore these a little more closely:

Head Knowledge Phase – Ages 6-25 – 19 years! For such a sharp lady, sure seems like I'm a bit slow sometimes, huh? I was raised in a Baptist church for most of my life and I walked that church aisle and gave my life to Jesus at the tender age of 6. I was soon baptized and pretty much sat in Sunday School and church 3 times a week up to the time I married at age 18.

Looking back at that phase in my life, I just breathe a sigh of relief to know that God is so good and that He obviously takes very good care of ignorant Christians. I did not have the slightest clue how to choose God's perfect will (like in my choice for a husband, career, or children) for my life but miraculously God guided me through many stupid mistakes and brought very good things into my life.

Although I would have my spurts of seriousness over my faith, basically I was self-absorbed and just busy with life without including much of Jesus. It was during this phase of my walk that I met and married a wonderful man, Michael Keith Clemons, completed the work on my Masters of Business Administration degree, and gave birth to two beautiful babies – Tyler Godfrey Clemons and Emily Michael Clemons…

After Mike and I met and married we were not faithful in our church attendance. Mike had been raised Catholic but his family was far away so when we did attend church, he would always go with my family and me to my Baptist church. I thought Mike was a Christian when we married. I just assumed, I guess, since he had a strong religious background. However, one night a little bit into our marriage I remember lying in bed with him and asking him about prayer and forgiveness. It quickly became apparent that he didn't have a personal relationship with Jesus Christ at all.

I was 25 when our daughter arrived, and we both began to feel the need to make church a real part of our life and to make sure our children had the benefit (as we did) of faithful church attendance, so we quickly began to attend a local Baptist church more faithfully.

<u>Shirt-tail Phase - ages 25-35 – 10 years</u>. I'm getting quicker! This phase begins with Mike accepting Christ as his Lord and Savior and the dramatic impact this immediately had on our whole family's life. Mike was always a good person who was kind and helpful to all people in his life so that part of him didn't change much. However, he had a degree in Biology and Chemistry and had a very scientific mind about him. Finding God put an amazing spin on his thinking and he just couldn't get enough study time in Scripture and commentaries. Mike would intensely

listen to the sermons and he asked questions galore at all times. He had a hunger and a desire to know all he could about God.

On top of this desire to learn, Mike also had a very people-oriented personality, extremely gregarious! He was a tall guy with a large frame so even his physical presence was larger than life. Combine that with his totally uninhibited manner with people and he always reminded me of John the Baptist in the Bible. Everywhere we went, he was talking to and making friends with people and sharing the Good News.

Mike immediately became very involved in our church and he was soon teaching classes and in charge of the bus ministry at times. I also was serving on a small scale in the church but most of my church-time activities involved caring for our kids and following John the Baptist around.

During this phase in my life, my career really took off. The semester before I received my Master's degree, I was hired to teach 12 hours for a small junior college. This was a great job for me and a good way to build my professional credibility. After three and a half years of teaching, I moved on to work with the Cherokee Nation.

Within just one year at Cherokee Nation, I doubled my salary and had been hired as their Economic and Business Development Director. This was a big job and kept me traveling and constantly hopping. My two oldest kids were also getting involved in lots of school activities and I was very focused on helping them be successful. Obviously, for about 8 years of that life phase, I was going through the motions of serving God but I had a tremendous amount of things in my heart to crowd out Jesus.

The last two years of this life phase involved a shift in our family's thinking. To use an old management term, Mike and I experienced a paradigm shift in our family.

This was a slow process and is more complicated than I can quickly go into here, but I think the busier I became in my work the more he and I realized that we, mostly me, were chasing things that weren't the best for our family.

About that same time, we had decided to have another child and our Mason Thomas was quickly on the way. About 5 months into the pregnancy, the Cherokee Nation experienced a particularly difficult tribal election and I was the very visible tribal director who was on the losing side of that election gone sour. I quickly resigned and found myself as a full-time mom.

It was during this process that we began to home-school our children, and we were working hard to make God the center of our home. I quickly moved into overdrive trying to be "earth mom" and was grinding wheat for bread and I got into mega frugal shopping techniques, etc. Seems like nothing I ever decide to do is small! I wanted to be the very best stay-at-home mom possible.

I was also now working hard on my relationship with God, and He was manifesting more and more of Himself within my heart and actions as I opened the door and gave Him the opportunity… It was also during this time that Mike was diagnosed with mouth cancer.

Mike's illness is a story in itself and I've included a full chapter about it, and his treatments, later in the book. From the time Mike was diagnosed with a small white bump on the side of his tongue until he went to be with the Lord was a quick 11-month process and it swiftly pushed me into life phase #3.

<u>Widowed or rules, rules, and more rules.</u> Phase 3 began March 6, 1998 and continued for 3.5 years. This stage of my life is characterized by two primary realities:

1) Making Jesus Christ the actual Lord of my life!

2) Rules - Being motivated to serve God primarily out of fear and guilt.

I was obviously getting much closer to sweet fellowship with my Lord during this life stage but Satan used the fear and guilt that I was experiencing over Mike's illness and death to "twist" my perception of God and how I related to Him. This basically resulted in a very out of balance approach to serving God and thinking that the Christian walk was trying hard to fit into a very small description of how a "perfect" Christian and Christian family looked and acted.

This was the phase of my life that most of this book is written about. As I said earlier, I think that if God could have favorites it would be widows and fatherless children because my children and I have story after story of God's powerful hand of provision and blessing moving in our lives!

Toward the end of this stage and after another huge tragedy in my life, I met a carpenter who introduced me to "new and refreshing" thoughts about my Lord and Savior.

Not long after I began to wonder if there was "more" to God than I had ever realized, I traveled with a lady to Washington, D.C. for a business conference. During the course of that week, she also shared new insights and invited me to visit her church to learn more. The decision to "check out" this church moved me into my current life stage.

Freedom – Falling in Love with Jesus. The churches I had grown up with taught 95% salvation messages – they were great at getting people saved but not so great at giving people very practical solutions for the problems they faced in life. Many times my church would do a wonderful job describing the problems but did not effectively outline how to solve those problems. The thing I thought I was missing in my walk with God up to this point was finding a place where I could receive God-led and Scripture laden information that I could apply every day and see dramatic results in my life. This was exactly what I found at Cornerstone Fellowship and my life has never been the same.

Thinking about how Cornerstone "tweaked" my thinking about God reminded me of verses in Isaiah 29: 10-13, "For the Lord has poured out on you the spirit of deep sleep, and has closed your eyes, namely, the prophets; and He has covered your heads, namely, the seers. The whole vision has become to you like words of a book that is sealed, which men deliver to one who is literate, saying, "Read this, please." And he says, "I cannot, for it is sealed." Then the book is delivered to one who is illiterate, saying, "Read this, please." And he says, "I am not literate." "<u>Inasmuch as these people draw near with their mouths and honor Me with their lips, but have removed theirs hearts far from Me, and their fear toward Me is taught by the commandment of men</u>, Therefore, behold, I will again do a marvelous work among this people, a marvelous work and a wonder;

for the wisdom of their wise men shall perish, and the understanding of their prudent men shall be hidden."

In these passages of Scripture, (this is my "mini" version of the story) the prophet is telling the people that they are blind and deaf to the vision placed before them – they can't see God's perfect will because they are only honoring God with their mouth, and their hearts are full of man-made rules and regulations. I think this adequately describes where I was prior to realizing the freedom I had in serving God and really falling in love with Jesus.

After God walked me through many "new" realities about Himself in this new church atmosphere, I was again faced with a situation in my life. This circumstance was one where I had to make a very deliberate choice of whether I would FULLY serve my God or allow a relationship to erode my fellowship with my Savior. I've always heard that Christians will come to points in their walk where God is asking them to “Die to Self” and this was one of those points in my life.

To make a long story much shorter, I chose God over this relationship and God then immediately impressed two very distinct things upon my heart. He told me to learn about prayer language and to stop focusing on myself and find my ministry in the Kingdom. Armed with that new directive, He led me to the most amazing discovery of my Christian walk. This discovery was such a sweet process and I look forward to sharing that discovery with you at the end of my story. It is my prayer that you will enjoy riding along with the story of my life and that it will paint a beautiful picture of a loving God who is actively involved with every step we take in this life!

Book Dedication - It is my hope that this book will serve two primary purposes:

First, I pray that in all things God is glorified and my readers will realize without a shadow of a doubt just how "REAL" God can be in someone's life once they hand him the throttle.

Secondly, it is my desire to honor my late husband, Michael Keith Clemons, for living a Godly life; for loving and cherishing me for 17 wonderful years; for leaving his four children a wonderful Godly heritage; and for being my biggest cheerleader among the great cloud of witnesses!

I can't wait to see you again someday, Mike. You received everything God promised you – thinking of you walking in the presence of God and among thousands and thousands of angels in joyful assembly takes away any tears that might still linger in my eyes. I'm so thankful that you made Jesus your Lord and Savior and that you were able to live such a victorious Christian life, however short it might have seemed.

Special Thanks – Although there are numerous people in my life that have positively contributed to the completion of this book, I want to single out two of my dearest friends in the whole wide world, Jay and Donna Jones, for their assistance. Jay, you were relentless and absolutely amazing with your editing efforts. Donna, you are the perfect friend in every possible way! Thank you for putting up with both Jay and I during this process.

Table of Contents

Remembering the Illness – an 11 month maze of choices

I will never forget the day that I was sitting on the couch in my living room and Mike came home early from work. He had just finished with a dentist appointment. He walked into the living room and with a serious expression on his face he told me that he had something that he wanted to talk about. He then sat down on the couch next to me and explained that at his dentist appointment the week before, the dentist had noticed a small white bump on the side of his tongue that evidently looked suspicious and he had taken a biopsy. Just now at the dentist he had been told the bump was actually cancerous and they had scheduled an appointment with a specialist in Tulsa to further investigate what was happening.

Talk about stunned! I just sat there looking at this big 'ole healthy looking guy who never had been sick a day in his life. How in the world could anyone think this guy could be sick, much less have a disease as serious sounding as cancer. When a person hears the big "C" word the first time, emotions just explode in your head. I had a million questions but Mike didn't have any answers. We just sat together on the couch awhile with me rubbing his arm and snuggling. After just a bit, Mike needed to get up and get himself busy so we just launched back into our regular life, pretty much ignoring what we had just been told.

Just a few days later, Mike went to see the doctor in Tulsa and surgery was quickly scheduled to remove the spot on his tongue. The doctor seemed very confident that the cancer had been caught early and that all would soon be back to normal in our lives. Toward the end of April

1997, Mike underwent his first cancer surgery at St. Francis hospital in Tulsa.

Mike was quite nervous before the surgery. As I said, he had never been sick a day in his life much less had surgery of any kind. To ease his mind, Mike and I spent quite a bit of time in prayer together before the surgery and our small Baptist church was a champion in praying for our family! Word quickly spread through the local communities and I know we had hundreds of people praying for Mike's successful surgery and a quick recovery.

Seeing God's love manifested in people's actions such as their intense concern and on-going prayers for our family really boosted our faith. God was so good to surround us with people who helped increase our faith in this scary time in our lives. In Hebrews 11:1 (NKJV), it states that faith is the substance of things hoped for, the evidence of things not seen. In Strong's Concordance #4102, faith is described as confidence, trust, belief, reliance, trustworthiness, and persuasion. In the New Testament, faith implies an inward confidence, trust, assurance, and reliance in God that He does all that He says He will do in His Word. Faith seems like such a simple process when described in this way, but in reality, and especially looking back on the early days of Mike's illness, faith became a very conscious choice – a choice we daily made to trust and have confidence in relying on God's promises.

The surgery didn't seem to last very long and I was thankful that my family and a deacon from our church had waited with me. The doctor met with me soon afterwards to assure me that all went well. He explained that they had continued to cut tissue around the cancer until they had achieved a "clean" margin all the way around it. He also explained that Mike's mouth had swelled more than they had expected so he was breathing with the aid of a trach tube in his throat. The doctor talked about Mike needing cancer treatments just in case to catch any lingering cancer cells that might be floating around in his body and he gave us a 96% survival rate. All in all it seemed like very good news to me!

Seeing him breathing through the trach tube after the surgery really surprised me. He looked like he was in such a serious condition, all those machines going and the sound of the air whizzing in and out through that tube was frightening. I gently rubbed Mike's forehead and tried to comfort him the best I could. I constantly was "shooting up" prayers for his quick recovery and I really felt peaceful believing that Mike would fully recover. I constantly held fast to verses like Hebrews 11:1 describing faith and sections in Scripture such as Matthew 6: 25-34 that beautifully describe God's tireless care and attention to the smallest detail in our lives. These Scriptures describe over and over again the process of fully relying on God, being confident that He wants to, and will, take care of our life's details, and the Scriptures are emphatic about NOT

WORRYING, which is a good lesson in life. Little things do matter to God and I believe that one of His greatest delights is when we fully rely on Him, for both the big and little in our lives.

Having Mike totally incapacitated and me carrying the load of the family on my shoulders was so different and difficult for me at this time in my life. Marrying young and then having a solid marriage where Mike fulfilled his role as the household leader meant this was all new territory for me. Little did I know that this was just the beginning of my new role in life.

Mike remained in the hospital about six days after the surgery and was gaining strength and feeling good. He was having trouble swallowing but had been able to breathe without the aid of the trach, although they kept it in place in case there might be more swelling. We set off for home with an optimistic attitude and an appointment to meet with an oncologist in Muskogee to begin the follow-up cancer treatments.

Mike felt good enough that he decided to just meet with the oncologist himself. I was operating a small little daycare out of my home for extra money and entertainment for Mason Thomas so I stayed home and worked during many of his early doctor's appointments. When Mike returned from that visit, he was scheduled to begin treatments in just two days and would continue the regimen as prescribed for the next 8 weeks.

In the beginning, the treatments seemed to be a breeze. However, it really didn't take much longer before he began to see harsh side effects. One of the first things that happened was the radiation killed his salivary glands and he no longer had saliva in his mouth. The treatments also made his throat VERY sore and this was complicated even more by the lack of liquid in his mouth. Both of these things combined meant that Mike was no longer able to effectively eat and he began to really lose the weight.

Well, we rocked along as best we could trying different kinds of liquid meal replacements to keep Mike nourished. He seemed to grow weaker and weaker and we both wondered if the treatments really were worth all the side effects. However, no one even talked about there being other options besides the surgery/treatment method of fighting cancer so we just continued forth.

The old Mike, the before cancer Mike, was full of life and passion. We had a good time in our marriage and Mike was always full of surprises. I began to really miss his old energy and health and he also would talk about how things were changing drastically for him. Around the 4th of July, I can remember that Mike had a day or so of really feeling good and we were able to enjoy one another like the old days.

Around the first of August I noticed something that I hadn't expected or even had thought about – I was late for my monthly cycle. I thought, "*No way, that's impossible, the doctors told us that the treatments would make Mike sterile.*" Well SURPRISE, we had our 4th child on the way.

Mike and I were elated with the news after we picked ourselves up off the floor! After our surprising news, I remember Mike standing up and making the announcement at our church. He proclaimed to the world that we had our 4th child on the way and that he was confident that this was a sign that God was healing him from this disease. Mike loved Scripture such as Psalms 127:3-5 – (NKJV) "Behold, children are a heritage from the Lord, The fruit of the womb is a reward. Like arrows in the hand of a warrior, so are the children of one's youth. Happy is the man who has his quiver full of them." He just knew that he would live to see all his children grow up and I believe he continued with that hope until the day he died. For both of us, it was just too impossible to think that we would have another child and Mike would die... there was just no way that could ever happen.

Well, the treatments ended finally and we moved along trying to get on with the business of life after cancer treatments and preparing for our new little addition. Although Mike had finished treatments, it just seemed he keep growing weaker and weaker. He was no longer able to sleep lying down because he would get a weird choking feeling in his throat. He no longer had any appetite at all and his throat remained so raw that even drinking the cold meal replacement shakes was next to impossible. Weight just continued to fall off of Mike – at this time he had probably lost close to 60 pounds.

I remember in October of 1997 saying to him that I felt there was more going on with his health than just being weak from the treatments. I encouraged him to visit his doctor again as soon as he could and get himself checked out again. Not long after this conversation, Mike started having horrible ear pain on one side. He thought he had a bad infection and made an appointment with his cancer surgery doctor in Tulsa to be referred onto a good ear, nose, and throat doctor.

Mike dashed off to Tulsa and came home a few hours later with an appointment to see a specialist in Oklahoma City. This new doctor in Oklahoma City was the most well known ear, nose, and throat specialist in the U.S. "Thank God," I thought, "at least we can seek out this specialist to investigate Mike's ear pain and we don't have to travel half way around the U.S. to find the very best."

Our appointment with the specialist was early that next week and I remember the long drive to Oklahoma City. My tummy was really beginning to grow and every mile along the way little Noah Benjamin squirmed around inside of me. We finally found the hospital and located the doctor's office and settled in to wait for our appointment.

Not long after that Mike was weighed and had his vitals taken and we were led into a waiting room. I remember the room was bigger than the usual exam room and the tools looked strange. Obviously this guy used some very specialized stuff in his examinations, I thought.

Well, the doctor soon arrived and after the introductions and a briefing over what had happened to Mike over the past seven months, he proceeded with the examination. I remember watching him as he looked inside of Mike's ear and then would press around on his jaw and neck, sort of toward the back of his jaw. He did this several more times; pressing and looking in his ear, and then he left the room. In a few minutes an assistant arrived with the doctor and the two of them pressed around on Mike's throat and jaw and look down inside of his ear once again. He then told us that we could meet in his office to talk. I thought, "*Hey, what's the deal, is that all there is to this expert examination?*"

The four of us met in the doctor's office and he quickly proceeded to tell us that Mike had a very large tumor growing in the floor of his mouth (probably about the size of a softball!) that extended out toward his right ear. This tumor was blocking the tubes in his ear and causing the pain. He went on to explain that when he pressed on the tumor in different locations he could actually see fluid from the cancerous tumor squirting up inside Mike's ear canal.

I just sat there stunned and began to cry. After explaining that information, the doctor said that because this was a recurrence of the original cancer, there was very little chance that Mike would now survive – the odds were about 20%. He looked so matter of fact as he told us all of this. It only took him a few breaths of air to basically tell us that Mike was dying and he couldn't help him.

Well, I immediately got very angry. I yelled at him asking if he had noticed that I was carrying a tummy that was very full of our 4th child and how in the world could he be telling me that Mike would probably die! I know my actions were totally uncalled for but he seemed to just be reading out of some medical journal with no emotion, not really talking to REAL people who needed to live. Mike quickly stepped in to “hush” me up and asked the doctor to overlook my emotion and to please give us more information about treatment alternatives. I got a grip on my emotions and just sat there in sheer disbelief as this guy continued to rattle on and on with his bad news.

The doctor then explained that there was a BIG surgery that could be performed on Mike. It would last about 24 hours and would involve several teams of doctors. He explained that this surgery would remove the tumor and even some tissue down into Mike’s shoulders, remove most of Mike’s tongue, and then a team of plastic surgeons would come in and try to reconstruct everything as much as possible. The doctor said that after the surgery, Mike would never speak again. He might have a small piece of tongue left but his speech would be terribly garbled. He also said that Mike would never again eat or drink through his mouth and probably would have to always use a trach tube for breathing. Worse still, there was a possibility that the surgery might not eliminate the cancer and he would have a very small chance to live.

The doctor and his assistant then said they would leave us alone to talk about the surgery between ourselves and would be back in a few to make plans if we chose to move forward with it. Well, as they left the room I still wasn't very calm but I was trying hard not to over-react and help Mike make a good decision.

As we sat there and discussed our choices, it was very apparent that Mike believed it made sense to go for the surgery and the possibility that God would use this method to rid his body of this awful disease. So I jumped on board and we then made arrangements for all the pre-surgery tests that needed to be performed.

In a few days, we were back in Oklahoma City for tests so they could see if the cancer had invaded any other areas in his body besides his head and neck area. I remember waiting around for a few hours for the test to be read and then waiting outside the doctor's office again for him to read the results for us. As we sat there, we prayed together and Mike told me that he was convinced that when they read the x-rays the cancer would be gone – he would be miraculously healed of this disease. I quickly agreed.

Well, the time came for that test review and an entire team of people met with us, probably about 10 or more. During the course of the discussion, they all confirmed that the tumor was probably even larger than originally thought but as far as they could tell, the cancer hadn't spread to any other part of Mike's body. However, until they removed the lymph tissue in Mike's neck and shoulder area they couldn't be certain. The team then recommended that the surgery was worth trying and we both agreed to move forward with the process. We had about one week to prepare for this experience.

Once back home, I tried so hard to get Mike to prepare for losing his speech. I wanted him to make individual tapes of his voice for me and the children; I wanted to talk to him about his thoughts about death. I wanted to understand about his life insurance and retirement benefits. I wanted to plan for all eventualities, to name his baby... and help me plan our future just in case it didn't include him.

Well, all of that talk only frustrated Mike. He told me that talking about those sorts of things showed a lack of faith that he would be healed and he refused to play that game. I felt ashamed for wanting to have a "just in case" plan so I agreed to charge forward without doubts of losing him – or at least this is how I kept it on the surface to honor his wishes.

The night before the surgery we didn't sleep much and just lay in bed holding hands and praying most of the night. We asked God over and over again to heal Mike. Just a few days before, our church had called the elders together and had anointed Mike with oil and prayed with him. Before this occurred I had shown Mike the Scriptures in James 5: 14-15 that say "Is anyone among you sick? Let him call for the elders of the church, and let them pray over him, anointing him with oil in the name of the Lord. And the prayer of faith will save the sick, and the Lord will raise him up. And if he has committed sins, he will be forgiven." Although this wasn't a common practice for our Baptist church, they concurred the Scriptures were very clear on how to proceed when someone was sick and they agreed to perform this ceremony and to allow God any way possible to bring healing into Mike's life.

When I look back on the anointing service, I'm certain that the experience was very powerful for all the deacons and elders involved. There wasn't a dry eye in the house as they finished praying over Mike. I firmly believe God used that experience to change many lives that day, much as God has used Mike's story over and over again to encourage people and strengthen their faith.

On the day of the surgery, Mike and I left home about 4:00 a.m. for the two-hour drive to Oklahoma City. The drive was pretty quiet between us. Mike was extremely nervous and didn't much feel like talking so I just chose to sit quietly hugging my tummy and praying. Once at the hospital, things moved pretty quickly as they prepared for this huge surgery ordeal.

Mike's mother, Colleen, met us at the hospital and within an hour they took Mike away to begin putting him to sleep. Colleen and I settled into the waiting room for the more than twenty-four hour wait.

Every hour or so, the doctors would call the waiting room and give me an update as to what was happening. Most of the surgery went smoothly but the tumor was larger than they expected so its removal was very time consuming.

A little over 24 hours later, the doctors came in to announce the surgery was complete and they were going to move Mike into intensive care. I quickly walked out into the hallway as they were wheeling Mike toward the Intensive Care unit and I'll never forget what he looked like laying there on that gurney. He actually looked dead! I guess they had slowed his heart rate and kept him ice cold during the procedure because he had a slight bluish tint to his skin and was freezing cold to the touch. He was on a ventilator and the artificial motion of that machine moving his chest in and out was disturbing.

Once Mike was inside the Intensive Care unit, I was able to go in and see him. The doctors then explained to me that they would keep him sedated and on the ventilator until later that morning so I should just try to go home and get a few hours sleep because he would not know I was there anyway. I rubbed his arms and hand awhile and then agreed to go to Mike's sister's house, just a few miles away, and sleep for a few hours.

After a restless few hours, I awoke and Mike's sister and brother-in-law took me back to the hospital. When I walked in early that morning, Mike was awake. His eyes were intensely focused on me and I could see that he was in major panic. I can't really explain why, but when I looked into his eyes, I just knew he needed my help. I don't think he had been awake very long but the hospital was slowing allowing him to breathe on his own, weaning him off the ventilator.

After Mike caught my eyes, he looked sharply toward his arms which were under the covers. I quickly walked over and lifted the sheet off his arms. When I did,

I saw they had him strapped to the bed with Velcro straps, which I quickly untied. When his arms were free, he had the most gracious and sincere expression in his eyes. I gave him a kiss and stroked his forehead and he immediately went back to sleep…

That moment, I began to realize how helpless Mike would be for a while. That experience also was the beginning of me reading Mike's mind. Because he never was able to speak intelligently again, I constantly had to read his mind and listen through the garbled talk to figure out what was wrong and how to help him. I felt comforted knowing I had known how to help him that day. He almost looked peaceful as he lay there sleeping that morning.

The hospital brought in a rollaway cot and I spent several nights right beside Mike in the Intensive Care unit. I constantly received an enormous amount of attention because you must remember that I was extremely pregnant. I'm a tall lady (5'10") but I am very short waisted so when

I'm pregnant, my middle really sticks out. Also, my babies are very large (my third child weighed over 11 pounds) so that just intensifies how pregnant I look. By all indications this fourth baby, Noah Benjamin as Mike had already named him, would be just as large as his older brother.

Once in a regular room, things got easier. Mike steadily improved and we were learning how to care for the permanent trach tube in his throat. We had a suctioning machine (sounded like a personal vacuum cleaner) and we had to keep this with us at all times. Because of the extensive surgery, Mike's body was producing lots of fluids and these had to be suctioned off regularly to keep him from choking. The whole process was very disgusting because once suctioned, the thing had to be cleaned out. Sitting here tonight typing out this part of the story, my stomach is still turning. The smell and look of cancer is something you will never forget once that disease has invaded your life.

Mike stayed in the hospital for about two weeks. My two year old was really missing us and my family would bring him to see us fairly regularly. I was doing a good job caring for Mike so the doctor finally agreed to let us go on home. I had to contact the electric company and have our home placed on their critical list because Mike would need electricity constantly available to run the suctioning machine.

The drive home was scary. Mike's head had started healing in a downward sort of way so he looked down at the floor all the time. He was also still very swollen so he had the appearance of a big cartoon, his head and neck twice or more the normal size. Later we found out that Mike should have had constant physical therapy to allow him a nice range of motion in his neck but no one ever mentioned this to us at all. When we left, they scheduled us to come back to Oklahoma City in two weeks for a checkup.

Once we arrived home, our family began to try to live as normally as possible with this person that obviously was not doing very well. Mike was never able to lie down again so he spent 95% of his time sitting upright in a recliner trying to rest and sleep. I have never seen anyone who looked quite so uncomfortable all the time. I stayed close to Mike's side constantly, still trying to teach my older two children, and keep up with Mason and my growing tummy.

Our family and friends all sort of faded away during these last few months of the disease. I'm still not exactly sure why but I know part of it was that Mike was a very private person about how odd and disgusting this disease had made him. He probably wasn't very much into company and the people could probably sense this about him. Also, just seeing someone in that kind of pain and distress would be hard. I don't blame people for not wanting to come around.

Well, we whizzed through several doctor's appointments the next month or so and around the first of the year, the specialist in Oklahoma City suggested they perform another cat scan, plus several other tests, to see if the cancer had been eliminated. We met in Oklahoma City for the tests just like before and met later in the day with the doctor. He told us that it would take a couple of days to really evaluate the material gathered and he would phone us at home with the test results.

Two days later, I was in the bathtub taking a much needed bubble bath when the phone rang. My daughter answered it and she turned to her Dad to say the Oklahoma City doctor's office was on the line. Mike quickly brought the phone to me so I could find out what was happening.

The doctor started in his 'ole so famous way of just laying it straight on the line without emotion or hesitation. He quickly told me that the disease had spread to several areas all around Mike's body and that he had no further hope – there weren't any additional treatments or surgery that would help Mike – it was just a matter of time now.

I immediately hung up the phone and began crying so hard and fast that I couldn't catch my breath. Mike walked back into the bathroom about that time and obviously he could tell the news was not good. I blurted out to him, "He said it's everywhere and that it's over!" I then pointed to my huge tummy sticking up out of the bubbles and asked him how in the world could this be happening to us, how could we be having a new baby and Mike dying all at the same time. Mike's eyes just teared up and he quickly sat down on the closed toilet seat with his head sunk deeply into his hands.

I struggled so many times during his illness with being in the position where I needed to be comforting Mike, just like the scene in the bathroom (he was the one in pain and dying!), but then I would think about my pregnancy and trying to raise 4 children alone and I would quickly get into the "self pity" mode. For a long, long time after his death, I really struggled with those emotions. I wish I could sit here and write story after story of how I never let my "true" emotions shine and I always put Mike's needs first, but that would be a lie.

I was however a good wife to Mike – I handled lots of details during his illness, was tirelessly at his side helping him make decisions, praying with him, supporting him in trying new ideas – anything to make him feel like he was being proactive in fighting this disease. God has reminded me a few times directly and many times through close friends of mine that I responded to and acted in a loving way with Mike most of the time, how I totally fulfilled my marriage vows in sickness and in health, and stood by him supporting and loving him until he drew his very last breath. By and large, I have nothing to feel bad about. The ordeal with Mike losing his life at such a young age is just a product of this evil world we live in. Because God cannot have His perfect way in an imperfect world, sometimes - bad things just happen to good people.

I struggled for years in my faith to reconcile inside myself how I thought God could allow Mike to die, especially in light of him having such a young family to raise and lead. For a long time, I thought God's hand was directly involved in his death and that for whatever reason He had ALLOWED Mike to die, which I now definitely know was a lie straight from satan.

I truly believe that God is all knowing and all powerful and is everywhere at all times but now I also understand that because sin entered this world thousands of years ago, this world has become a very imperfect place and is NOT anything like God originally intended. Until Jesus returns someday, the world is rocking along and in that process bad things occur because of the sin around us. We are not puppets and God does not have full control of the sinful circumstances in our world.

I do think that most of the time when bad things happen it is because we have brought it upon ourselves in some way. If a person continually smokes then gets cancer, I don't think anyone could blame God in that situation. Junk just happens sometimes and in this instance for whatever reason, my husband became ill and did not survive. God is not the author of evil, only good. God is good ALL THE TIME, not just part of the time, and I will never blame Him again for the tragedy that occurred in our lives.

A few days after that conversation with the Oklahoma City doctor pronouncing Mike's case hopeless, a friend told me about a Christian doctor in Tulsa who used all natural therapies and radical new treatments to fight disease. I quickly talked to Mike about this alternative medical approach and we made an appointment. In a couple of days, we headed off to Tulsa to visit with this new doctor and gather his opinion on what if anything could be done to help Mike. In the interim, I had bought and borrowed many good books on the subject of alternative medical treatments. Mike and I were excited to realize that there was such a new and sensible approach to fighting disease that appeared much better than the cut, burn, and poison efforts that we had already tried.

After a thorough examination by this new doctor, Mike was started on several new regimens that were designed to rid his body of toxins and infused his system with mega amounts of vitamins to help him fight the disease. This new doctor was also very critical of the way the other doctors had chosen to fight the illness and how much damage this had caused Mike's body.

While we were at his office, he gave us information about a hospital in Tijuana, Mexico where they practiced the same routines he was recommending plus lots of other alternative therapies that the FDA had not given approval for in the U.S. He recommended that we contact this hospital and see if they could quickly treat Mike in a last ditch effort to save his life. After a frantic bout of plane reservations, packing, and gathering money, we quickly prepared to leave for a month long stay in Tijuana.

I’m so sorry

“I’m so sorry, I’m so sorry, Mike, I’m so sorry… I repeated the phase over and over to myself and screamed it to the heavens. I couldn’t quit saying I’m sorry. Friday, March 6th will forever be burned into my memory…

All around me for the past three days were strangers and unfamiliar words and lifestyles. The beach was dirty, the food was nasty, and Mike didn’t seem to be trying to live. I couldn’t help feeling disappointed in our surroundings because the mental picture I had formed while still in Oklahoma about this innovative cancer treatment hospital was not what I saw standing before me in Tijuana. The moment we crossed the border after landing in San

Diego on March 3, 1998, I began to feel we had made a mistake.

We landed in San Diego at about 11:00 and the airline had a wheelchair waiting for Mike just outside of the plane's exit. We gathered our luggage and looked for the driver who was to take us to the hospital. The hospital had made all the arrangements for us at the last minute and assured us that a driver would be waiting to whisk us away for miraculous healing treatments destined to cure even the sickest cancer victim. "There he is," I thought with relief when I saw the small Mexican man standing holding a sign that said "Michael Clemons Family," and we boarded the little bus. Also riding the hospital bus was one other family heading for cancer treatment just across the border. As we all sat there in silence, I looked at the other couple and tried to imagine what type of illness had invaded their family. The other mother on that Mexican bus was thin and pretty and the couple had two children, a boy and girl, about 5 and 7. The father looked tired and had that all too familiar sallow complexion of someone fighting cancer. I guessed he was probably suffering from some type of liver or lung cancer. He was able to walk and speak and seemed in good spirits as he and his wife quietly talked and held their children.

When that other couple looked across at our family, they probably felt grateful for their situation just for a moment. On our side of the hospital bus sat two children, one an active two-year old boy and the other a beautiful 10 year-old girl. Next to the children was a father unable to speak, thin and pale, unable to eat, and barely able to hold up his head. The tongue cancer had spread throughout his head and neck region and through the surgeries and cancer treatments his head had fused in a downward manner that made him look at the floor. His jaws were greatly swollen and his lips protruded in a weird sort of pout. Mike looked gruesome to say the least. He had to lean far back and strain his eyes to look straight out at the world. Next to the father, and holding the two-year old, the other family would have seen me - the Mom. I would have grabbed their interest and attention because I was carrying a huge tummy that was full of our fourth child, Noah Benjamin who was due March 27, 1998.

Tijuana, Mexico was a nasty place. Poverty was everywhere and I kept thinking, "*How in the world can a place like this have an amazing hospital worth $14,000 cash?*" As we pulled into the hospital parking lot I kept having a sick feeling rising in my throat and wondering if we had made a mistake. Mike, though, was grateful for this opportunity. Our American doctors had told us that nothing else could be done, so we had researched and decided to try this all natural/mega-vitamin therapy approach to see if his cancer could be eliminated. Mike wasn't able to communicate very effectively, but he had voiced his gratefulness to me right before we left the United States.

He was thankful that I had agreed to "try anything" and had taken the bull by the horns to make the arrangements, secure flights, pack, make arrangements for our 15-year old son who wasn't coming along, gather the $14,000, etc. Mike had asked me if I thought we should try the Mexican treatment center and I said, "Sure, if you want to try it, we will try it." When I look back now, I'm so thankful that I agreed to go to Mexico even though the outcome was less than perfect. Knowing that I enabled Mike to feel a certain amount of peace for being proactive in curing his illness is a comfort to me now.

When we checked into the hospital, the first thing they wanted was the $14,000 cashier's check. We had not even seen a doctor or our room and I was furious. All my life I had been known for my ability to fight. I had always been outspoken and aggressive and this instance was no different. I refused to hand over the money until we had at least spoken with a doctor. The other family quickly handed over their check and quietly moved on to unpack and settle in their room. We, however, were moved to a small holding room and waited to speak with hospital representatives. Later, after less than satisfactory talks with several people, I reluctantly handed them our payment for the 4-week treatment and we moved into our room.

Four Days in Tijuana

To say that I wasn't a happy camper is to underestimate the self-pity and anger that was welling up inside me about the situation. Maybe the hospital knew what they were doing, maybe they didn't, but all I knew is that I was tired and scared and unsure of the quality or outcome of our month long visit.

To make matters worse, my two-year old, Mason Thomas, was very curious and active and kept me hopping. Although my 10-year old daughter was great to keep him corralled and busy, the strain of trying to keep a toddler happy in a hospital environment is awesome. Looking back at the decision to bring along our two-year old, I see that it was a big mistake. Even though he would have missed us during the month-long stay for treatment, this definitely was not a situation for a small child.

The week began with the hospital performing many tests on Mike and starting him on intravenous mega-vitamin supplements. Tuesday and Wednesday were spent assessing his current physical condition and we met with them on Thursday to hear their recommendations. They suggested physical therapy to enable him to lift and hold his head at the proper angle, full-blown doses of all vitamins, and a meeting with the dietitian later that day to decide the best way to avoid further weight loss. They also said that Mike was in much worse condition than they originally had thought from the phone conversations and voiced concern over the strong treatments he had already endured in the States which they considered to be detrimental to his healing. One comment voiced was, "We wish you had come to us first, before your husband was cut, poisoned and burned in the States." This thought made us feel hopeless and angry.

All throughout Tuesday and Wednesday, Mike's head and neck had begun to swell. They became enormous and there were spots on his neck and shoulders that began to ooze a thick dark fluid, almost like he was exploding. The doctors assured us that this was a good sign. They said his body was eliminating the internal poisons as quickly and efficiently as possible and sometimes this involved eruptions in the skin. I called home to Oklahoma to relay the good news that the treatments were working and Mike's body was trying to heal itself by releasing the poisons built up by treatments and the disease.

The hospital was touted for its all-natural approach to healing, so the food served was organic and vegetarian. They even took the pure food concept one step farther and served only raw vegetables, saying the cooking process eliminated much-needed vitamins. The hospital diet, known as the "Hallelujah Diet," was based on the premise that God had originally intended for man to eat only raw fruits and vegetables and it was only after sin entered the world that man began to eat meat and cook his food. This sounded as reasonable as anything else to us at this point so we happily complied.

Mike was fed through a stomach tube so pure doses of raw veggies and fruit were no problem for him. He had always been a meat and potato man and avoided most green things like the plague. It was a constant family joke to talk about him now being a vegetarian. Back at home, he or I had been preparing a blender full of food and vitamins about six times a day to try to keep him from losing more weight. His being thin seemed so odd to me. Mike was a very large man who was 6'3" tall and at times weighed as much as 275 pounds. In the eleven months since his diagnosis, Mike had lost 100 pounds.

After lunch on Thursday, I talked Mike into taking a walk to look at the Pacific Ocean. Mike had never seen the Pacific and I thought it might help the situation if we could all get out together and get some air. Though the beach was only about 2 blocks from the hospital the walk seemed like an eternity once we began. Mike was tightly hugging his coat around him because the weight loss had made him unusually susceptible to temperature and he was always cold. This was quite a point of contention between us because being nine months pregnant and 50 pounds heavier, feeling cold was not a problem for me.

The streets of Tijuana were depressing to say the least. Dirty food vendors sat along the street in front of the beach trying to make a few dollars. I wondered if people really did buy food from dirty carts, but decided it must be profitable or they wouldn't be there.

I will never forget watching Mike look at the ocean that day. He leaned as far back with his legs as possible (it almost looked like he was trying to do a backbend) so he could elevate his eyes to the point where he could get a good look at the water. He had the most incredulous look in his eyes and I even thought I might have seen a grin deep in his mangled face.

The beach was dirty like everything else and the water was furious. The sand was dark and there were lots of jagged rocks all along the coast. The beach was also filled with hundreds of sea gulls, which interested my two-year old immensely. Mason had always been a very verbal child and was able to speak loudly and clearly on almost every issue. He ran up and down the beach that day screaming, “Chickens! I’m going to catch you chickens!” I guess the old saying is true: you can take the kid out of Oklahoma, but you can’t take Oklahoma out of the kid.

An hour or so later when we finally made our way back to the hospital, Mike was more exhausted than I think I had ever seen him. He settled into his recliner and began his vitamin drip once again, quickly falling asleep. Mike was only able to sleep in an upright position since his last surgery the November before. Lying down made him unable to breathe properly so he had made an art out of dozing upright. He always looked so miserable to me trying to sleep this way. As I look back now, I can see this was a small blessing in disguise. We had been married for almost 17 years and in the course of that amount of time a person gets very used to having another body next to them in bed. However, with Mike's condition, I had already become accustomed to solo sleeping before his death, which probably made the transition to widowhood a slight bit easier.

Later on Thursday, the physical therapist came to our room and began to assess Mike's fused neck condition. Language was a barrier the whole time we were in the hospital and the conversation with this doctor was no different. Although she could speak English, it was difficult to have an intense conversation about the subject. What I did immediately understand from her was the fact that she was furious the doctors in the U.S. had allowed him to heal in such an awful position and she wanted to know why they hadn't given him intensive physical therapy immediately after the last surgery. I had no good answers and was once again feeling helpless for not knowing that I should have insisted on physical therapy. She then began to work with Mike.

It is hard to think about this time even now over five years later. When the therapist forcibly moved Mike's head up and down trying to create flexibility and a normal condition, it created extreme pain. If Mike could have screamed he would have. He had tears in his eyes and a look of torture that I will never forget. The therapist worked with Mike for about 30 minutes and said she would be back late on Friday for another session. Mike missed that appointment.

After the therapy session, the dietitian met with us to discuss Mike's new diet regimen. Because of his continual weight loss, the dietitian suggested we double his intake of food. On the surface this sounded reasonable, so beginning with breakfast on Friday morning, Mike began receiving about twice the usual amount of blended food.

Mason had been unusually active and cranky on Thursday evening and by the time he and his sister were finally asleep, I was not in a good mood. As I lay there in the uncomfortable bed shifting my enormous tummy trying to get comfortable, I was looking across the room at my sleeping husband. Actually, every time I looked across the room I saw the same thing - he was oozing, swollen, and asleep. Most of the time I just let the emotion roll past me, but on this night I chose to get angry.

Since our arrival on Tuesday, Mike had begun to swell and was sleeping more than ever. The hospital insisted that family accompany the patient during the

4-week treatment because there was a constant need to administer this medicine and that therapy. It was a full-time job to make sure the shark cartilage was taken at 11:00 and the coffee enema was performed two hours later and on and on. My thoughts were that Mike should be proactive in his care and keep himself mentally alert enough to make sure he was performing the medical regimen as prescribed. In my way of thinking, I had my hands full with two children and my pregnancy. This sounds incredibly selfish now, but at the time it was very real to me.

As the anger and fright rose in my chest, I proceeded to let it spill out on Mike. I cried and shouted and let him know that he didn't act like he even wanted to live. I wanted to know why he wouldn't pay attention, stay awake more, and deal with his schedule so I could properly deal with the children. I can remember asking him the question, "What would happen if I went into early labor and needed assistance? Could he be there for ME? Could he wrestle Mason until I was able to do so?"

I asked him for answers that I know he didn't have. As I look back on my temper tantrum, I'm filled with such shame and embarrassment that I took a situation that shouldn't have been about me and made it all about me and my comfort. I have only told two of my closest friends about this long conversation that Thursday night and both have insisted that I am being too hard on myself. However, I don't believe that I am probably hard enough in my analysis of my behavior.

My fit went on for hours it seemed but probably actually only lasted an hour or so. I had told Mike that I didn't see how I could possibly stay in Tijuana for the whole 4 weeks in that small room trying to wrestle Mason and dealing with no entertainment or proper food for a child. The hospital did not serve separate meals for the families, so everyone had only fresh fruit and vegetables to eat. Mason wasn't eating and was not sleeping well either with everyone crammed into the one room. I was also very frightened of going into labor so far away from home and not having anyone to help me. In my own assessment, I behaved like a frantic spoiled brat.

Finally, sleep and I found one another. The next morning, Friday March 6th, I opened my eyes and immediately saw Mike gazing at me. I will never forget the look in his eyes as he began to speak. Because of the extensive surgeries and the swelling, it was next to impossible for anyone to understand him but me. I guess because we had been around one another for over 17 years, I could read between the lines and figure out what he was saying. He apologized for my anguish and said, "I spent the whole night talking to Jesus about our situation and everything will work out fine." He said that we could talk about it later, but once again reassured me that all would work out. I felt better and it seemed to be a natural situation once again with him protecting me. Just then, the nurse arrived with Mike's "double portion" of breakfast and we began our day.

Friday was better for us. Mike was staying awake more and taking charge of his routine. I felt relief that he was "taking the bull by the horns" and facing the situation as a fighter. You see, to me a person who doesn't fight is weak and weakness was not a trait that I could tolerate. It lifted my spirits and mood to know he was trying.

When I think back on most of the day that Friday, nothing comes to mind except Mike's new resolve to stay awake and participate, so the day must have been fairly non-eventful. Lunchtime came around and Mike received a double portion once again. The kids and I took another walk to the beach after Mason's nap and we arrived back at the room right before dinnertime, probably about 4:30 p.m. Tijuana time.

The kids and I were always hungry before meals because our stomachs were still on Oklahoma time. For this reason, we were usually always the first ones in the dining room. I'm not really sure why, because the thought of eating more salad with yogurt dressing was not at all appetizing to me. Mason hated the food but Emily seemed to be enjoying it. Supper time tonight was no different than it had been the rest of the week and the kids and I were watching the clock for 5:00 to roll around so we could grab our supper in the downstairs dining room.

Right before 5:00, Mike began to cough and gag. He was always doing this type of thing and we had all become accustomed to disgusting sounds, fluids, and smells coming from his neck and mouth. This seemed no different than usual, expect Mason began to get sick. As Mike was gagging, it made Mason start to heave and I quickly whisked him out of the room so he wouldn't vomit. I said, "Come on, Emily, let's go ahead and go downstairs, they should be opening up for supper very soon." With these words, the three of us hurried out of the room with Mike coughing.

Once out of the room, Mason stopped heaving and we proceeded down to the dining room. A few other people were gathered in line already and we took our place behind them. We had waited just a couple of minutes when I remembered something I had left in the room and I sent Emily back upstairs.

A few minutes later, Emily was back screaming that Mike was in trouble and for me to come. She ran ahead of me and as I approached the room, I could see quite a crowd gathered. I ran into the room and saw Mike slumped on the floor with a doctor trying to hold him up by the shoulders. Mike was pale and limp and I could tell that he wasn't breathing. The doctor screamed for a gurney and they ran down the hall with Mike on a stretcher. Emily had apparently come back into the room and had seen her Dad choking. She said he was turning very blue and had motioned for her to get help. Emily then ran down the hall to get help and the nurses had a hard time understanding what she wanted but she finally got her point across and they called for more help.

Part of the next few minutes is a blur, but I'm pretty sure that another couple from the hospital gathered Emily and Mason and took them to their room. Emily and I still haven't had a long conversation about that night, but she did say that a crazy couple tried to keep them away from the action and that she finally forced her way past them with Mason in tow and went downstairs to the emergency room. I guess one of the nurses saw them and placed them in a room separate from me. I will never to this day understand why they didn't bring the kids to me but there we were, Mike in trouble, Emily and Mason in one room, and me in another waiting for someone to tell us what was happening.

I could hear lots of commotion going on in the emergency room but I couldn't see anything. I sat there in that dinky little room repeating over and over how sorry I was to Mike. All I could think of was that I had left him alone coughing and then choking and that he was now dying. I was overwhelmed with a feeling of guilt that I still can't completely shake even five years later.

Time passed so slowly and finally the doctor came into the room. He explained that Mike had vomited (I'm sure in part because of all the extra food he had been fed that day) and because he wasn't able to open his mouth fully (due to the swelling) that he had aspirated on the vomit and had stopped breathing. This in turn had caused his heart to arrest and he was now dead. As I type those words, my skin still tingles and words just can't adequately describe the feelings that flood over you in a circumstance such as that. I began screaming like a crazy woman and I know that everyone there expected me to begin labor any second. The doctors then led me into the room where Emily and Mason were sitting and I began to tell them that their Daddy was gone.

Emily immediately began trying to comfort me. She was rubbing my back while holding Mason very tightly and crying softly. I let her take the lead in comforting me just for a second, and I know that God spoke to my heart and said, "She is your child – you need to let her grieve." I told Emily that I was her Mommy and would take care of her. I said, "You can be the little girl and do what you need to do." As soon as she heard me say this, she started crying – crying out for her Dad. We spent awhile just holding onto one another with tears flowing.

A nurse came into the room after a short time and asked if we wanted to see Mike. I had peeked through the door before I was brought into the kids and had seen him lying on his back with tubes coming out of his mouth. They had probably tried CPR or shock to get his heart going because his shirt was open and the stomach tube had been cut. There was a little blood around the tube and I remember how thin he was. Lying there, it looked like the front of his stomach was just about three inches from his backbone. He looked like a living skeleton. I turned to Emily and asked if she wanted to see her Daddy and I will never forget her response. She said just as big and brave as any war veteran, "That is not my Daddy. My Daddy is in heaven now. He has his tongue back and he can talk!" With those words, the three of us rode the elevator back to the second floor to pack our things and then into our future without Mike.

Looking back on all the things that happened during Mike's almost year long battle with cancer, what always impresses me is how trusting Mike and I were of the recommendations being handed to us. Each step along the way, until actually the very end, we would meet with doctor after doctor and proceed forward thinking they were telling us information that would help. Looking back, though, I see that we made critical errors.

I will never look at being seriously ill the same again. Knowing what I know now, I would search diligently for non-invasive procedures up front, the kind that might have given Mike close to the same amount of time on earth but would have allowed him to be comfortable and enjoy more of his last days. Spending your final days on earth trying to recover from the surgeries and treatments that were meant to save your life is ridiculous!

The Adventure Really Begins…

Back in our second floor hospital room, I immediately phoned my Pastor with the news. Pastor Adrian was so sweet and comforting on the phone and I could tell how gut wrenching it was for him to be so far away from a member of his church who was in such need. He agreed to call my family and to be present when they talked with our oldest son, Tyler, who had stayed in the States with his Aunt Connie.

A whole lot of the next hour or so doesn't even register with me anymore. I spoke with my family, Mike's family, made emergency plane reservations to leave early the next morning from San Diego, and we began to pack and prepare to leave. I had the most overwhelming dread rising up inside of me about the shock of the ordeal throwing me into labor. The thought of giving birth in Tijuana, Mexico, with my two youngest children having no one to be with them just made my skin crawl. I had one thing on my mind and that was getting out of Mexico and back into the States.

I called the front desk to order a taxi to take us across the border and a representative from the hospital soon came to our room. She informed us that we were not allowed to leave because we needed to fill out the proper paperwork and sign releases from their attorney the next day. Can you guess that didn't sit too well with this determined "Mommie to Be?" My daughter also joined in the conversation and stated that we were leaving – with or without their help – and we weren't waiting to sign anything. I think back at how grown-up Emily was that day. Comforting her little brother for all that time alone in the emergency room, trying even to be the strong one for me after that, and now providing the back-up and encouragement I needed to stand strong and get out of Dodge.

Within about an hour and a half, we were on a bus heading back into the States. I told the driver to just take me to the motel nearest to the airport. It was really late by this time and I remember leaving my kids in the taxi and having to speak through a tiny bullet-proof window on the side of a little Mom and Pop motel. I explained our need for a room and she obliged by taking my credit card and giving me the keys. I kept thinking, *"I wonder if this lady can tell that I'm in the middle of the most horrible thing that has ever happened to me?"* I just kept wondering if my face reflected the experience that had occurred only a few hours before.

Once in the room, it was business as usual. Initially I was amazed that kids still needed baths, kids were hungry, and kids were still grouchy and unreasonable. Or, I guess you could say, kids are still kids. For just a second, I had the notion that they would realize that my heart had just exploded, that they would understand the need for complete silence and cooperation, and magically prepare their own selves for bed without hesitation or question. Dream on…

Bath time included me sitting in the floor and quietly washing Mason's little body and wondering how in the world I could show him how to grow into being a man by myself. I stretched over my huge tummy to grab him out of the tub and once again I became painfully aware of what I was facing. I would enter the hospital alone to give birth to Noah Benjamin. I would go to his Father's funeral with him in my tummy for all to see. I felt pathetic.

After Mason and Emily had their bath and snack, we talked a bit. I hugged them, reassured them, and prayed with them. They were keeping amazing control in the situation and I could tell they were taking their cues from me. I was "in control" and handling things just fine – they were too. Little did they know what was happening on the inside but I kept that deep inside until they were sound asleep.

I did not know that it was possible for a huge pregnant woman to lie on a hard floor, almost face down, and cry for an entire night. I was afraid that I would wake my children if I were in bed because I was shaking so hard. I sobbed such a deep and pitiful sob. It came from as far down in me as I had ever felt an emotion. During my time that night on the floor, I quickly began to realize just how much I now needed God and His provision. Although I had "head knowledge" of what it meant to be in total submission and in total reliance on God, I don't think that until that night it actually happened in my life. I'm not saying that I didn't have salvation before this experience; <u>I'm just saying that this night Jesus actually became the Lord of my life.</u> I was in complete 100% submission, broken, and I laid my life down at His feet.

Sleep did not happen for me that night or for several nights after that. We were up by 5:00 am heading to the airport with a month's worth of luggage in tow. I just kept having the same mental experience as I had the night before checking into the motel. Wondering over and over again if people we passed could see my anguish. Could they see my heart had broken and that I had just lost the love of my life? I still don't know why to this day that thought just kept coming into my mind over and over again.

As we boarded the plane, I began to dread the ride home. On the trip down to Mexico, my two-year old was "all wiggles." This was his first plane ride and as soon as the "keep your seatbelt on" sign went off, he was out of that seatbelt and all over the place. It was a constant hassle to make sure he wasn't bothering someone. As we settled into our seats, I prayed to God and said, "You've got to help me out here. I can't deal with this wiggly guy for 3 hours. Please do something." I then told Mason that a new rule had come to pass and he would not be allowed to take off his seat belt until we landed. He quickly said, "OK" and soon fell sound asleep. He woke up right before we landed in Oklahoma 3 hours later. This was just one of many miracles and answered prayers that lay in store for me and my family.

Sitting here tonight typing out this story for the first time, I'm reminded of a lady who was on our flight traveling to Mexico. Memories of this lady make me smile today because looking at that situation with a more enlightened attitude has really changed my life perspective. Anyway, there was this lady sitting behind us on the plane and she had one of those big infectious smiles – a person could tell she was a spirit-filled Christian lady and I knew she was NOT of Baptist persuasion but was one of those Charismatic-type Christians! People like that, when they were total strangers, always made me uncomfortable. I wasn't really sure if I was ready to say "Praise God" and pray for people at the drop of a hat. I guess it was the uptight little Baptist girl in me making a stand. This lady had noticed our situation. Boy was it obvious that we needed prayer. Me, all huge and pregnant, two kids, and a husband who looked like he had already died. Anyway, this lady pecked me on the shoulder and asked if she could pray for us, which she proceeded to do. She was passionate and bold and although I deeply appreciated her sincerity, I was not comfortable with her methods. I just didn't understand a person doing something like that for a total stranger.

Back in the States

My Dad and sister were waiting at the airport gate for us when we arrived at the Tulsa International Airport. My Dad is not usually one who shows much emotion, but this day was different. He whisked Mason up in his arms for a big hug and quickly took the "big strong Dad" approach – it made me feel a little bit better. My mother had stayed behind at home to field all the phone calls, food, and arrangements that needed to be made. All the way home on the plane, I had sat with a constant flow of tears streaming down my face. I wasn't sobbing or even making one single sound, but the tears were flowing so strongly that I couldn't even keep them wiped away. When I met my family at the airport, the tears finally stopped flowing for a time.

Driving home from the airport was non-eventful. I went through the story again of what had happened and our adventure getting out of the country so quickly. We just sort of all sat around in the car and discussed the issue like you would talk about a horrible story that happened to someone else. It still didn't feel real to me until my Dad asked me if I knew how we would get Mike's body home from Mexico. To everyone's surprise, I had NOT thought of how that would happen.

Once home, I quickly went into hibernation mode. Mike and I had built a home about one forth mile from my parents in the country right outside of Warner, Oklahoma. I told everyone that I didn't want to see or talk to anyone so it was decided that my parent's home would be the funeral headquarters and I would go to my house with my sister. Throughout this ordeal, my entire family was all so helpful but especially my sister Connie. I then showered and just went to bed. Connie wrangled Mason, and answered the phone and door if people had missed stopping at my parents. People came out of the woodwork with food, flowers, cards, money – it was unbelievable! The town almost immediately set up a Trust Fund at the local bank and money just poured into it.

Mike had always been a very gregarious fellow. I always teased him that every time we went into Wal-Mart he cornered some poor defenseless soul in the Parts or Sporting Goods Department and before we left the store, they would think they were his best friend. I'm not sure if the "high interest" level in helping us was brought on by his friendly nature, whether the story was just so sad and pathetic that people were drawn to help, or whether it was the hand of God pouring out blessing and provision. At some level, my guess is the public reaction was a bit of all three, but I immediately saw the hand of God begin to move mightily in our lives.

The next big thing on the immediate agenda was getting Mike's body back into the United States. I didn't know the details until much later because, like I said, I just shut down. I went to bed with my Bible and lay there praying and reading for most of the next few days. Later I learned that the Corps of Engineers top commander (Mike had worked for the Corps of Engineers for 20 years) out of Washington, D.C., had become involved and he had personally contacted the Mexican Embassy. Through the course of these top-level discussions, Mike's body was placed on an airplane and he arrived just a few hours before his funeral that next Thursday, March 12th – almost a week after his death. Thoughts of this brought a tiny little smile to my face as I would think about Mike and his pokey nature about getting places on time and how it could actually be said now that HE WAS ALMOST LATE FOR HIS OWN FUNERAL.

Mike was an early riser and was almost always up around 5:30 a.m. each day. He would spend huge amounts of time drinking coffee and on the computer with his online Bible program. Then, oh about 7:15 or 7:20, he would turn into "Maniac Mike" and try to get completely ready (showered and dressed) for work and leave by 7:30. Oh, and let's not forget, he almost NEVER could find everything he needed for his work uniform – tie, clips, badge, name plate, etc. I would hear him say, "Rhonda, do you know where my so and so is," and I'd always know. It was just second nature to pay attention to these things so I could assist in his frantic "getting out of the house" ordeal. His methods always amazed me. That was just part of what made Mike so unique. Me, well, if I had to leave by 7:30, I would hit the floor running at 6:30, fix breakfast, shower, dress, get the children completely ready, and I would be on the road maybe 5 minutes early. The old saying is true: Opposites really do attract.

Mike's family arrived early on the morning of the funeral – March 12th. His Mom, Dad, Brother, Sister, their family, and his Uncles all came. Everyone met at my parent's home and caravanned together to the service at Keefeton Trinity Baptist Church. Mike had been raised Catholic but was saved and baptized into the Baptist church after we were married. I was always a bit concerned how his family would respond to the Baptist funeral for their son.

My feelings were still very raw toward Mike's mother on that day. On the day he died, I called her myself right after I phoned my Pastor, which was my first phone call. Looking back on this, I can see now how calling his mother was a big mistake because of my emotional state. I was still reeling from guilt about leaving Mike alone while coughing; so on the phone I immediately started apologizing for leaving him alone and him dying. Her immediate response was, "You should have stayed with him – not left him alone, etc…" all in a very firm voice. Well, that wasn't exactly what I needed to hear at that particular time and I now realize that she was just in shock and grieving over the news that her oldest son was gone. It took me a long time to finally bury the anger I felt toward his Mom that day. I was in the middle of feeling like my life was breaking apart and all she had to add to the situation were "cutting words" that still bother me somewhat even today.

Standing in the Presence of the King

When we arrived at the church for the funeral, the parking lot was spilling over with people. There wasn't even enough room inside the church for everyone so people were in the foyer and the church hall. Pastor Adrian presented a wonderful service full of "Mike stories" about hunting, fishing, his INTENSE curiosity about Biblical issues, and his love for his family. He told several jokes that actually made me laugh. Emily was on my left and as soon as the service started, she turned to me and said, "I'm so sleepy" and she just lay down in my lap… her little system was shutting down because of all that was happening in her life. My oldest son Tyler was on my right. As we walked into the church that day, everyone stood up. A large group of Tyler's friends were right at the back of the church and when Tyler saw them he broke down. It was very difficult for everyone.

Emily had been taking voice lessons from a lady named Mary Kay Henderson. Mary Kay had this tremendous voice and I had asked her to sing at Mike's funeral. As she began the song, "Standing in the Presence of the King" there wasn't one dry eye in the house. A line in that song still stands out in my mind... all of a sudden I was standing in the presence of someone that I had never met but knew so very well...

Soon it seemed we were at the cemetery with my family and closest friends gathered around. It was a cold and windy day and as I sat there in the front of that group looking at Mike's casket, I felt like I was in a scene from a very bad movie. I had a crying child on each arm and a tummy full of my 4th child as I sat there thinking about Mike's life and how it had been cut so tragically short. That part of the funeral was the most difficult to me – there was just something cold and final about thinking how your loved one's body is about to be lowered into the earth for its final resting place. My comfort, though, through that awful experience was the mental picture of Mike in heaven, fully restored in a new body and in perfect peace and joy. I would imagine Mike time and time again chasing down all the old Bible saints to gather their viewpoints on all the questions that he had saved inside himself until he got to heaven... I could just see Mike talking with Moses, Paul, and John the Baptist. He was in his Father's house and singing with thousands and thousands of angels in joyful assembly. It's hard to stay sad when you have such a sweet picture in your mind after a loved one has passed on.

After the cemetery scene was over, my family and I went back to our church for a family lunch. Our church was full of precious ladies who would go above and beyond the call of duty to make a family feel comfortable and loved during a crisis. I really appreciated all their hard work that day. Completing the funeral marked the end of the "rushed activity" and it brought a sense of closure to the death experience for me. I was now ready to bring Noah Benjamin into the world, settle in, pour my heart and trust out to Jesus, and try to figure out how to raise my babies by myself.

Noah Benjamin makes his debut...

Because I was absolutely exhausted, my gynecologist scheduled to induce my labor about two and a half weeks after the funeral – March 24, 1998. Noah was a big baby anyway (his older brother had arrived on his birthday weighing in at over 11 pounds!) so everyone was anxious to get the birth behind us. My Mother, Sister, and Emily accompanied me to the hospital in Tulsa that morning very early.

I'm not sure how, but the entire hospital staff knew what had happened to my husband and the silence and tiptoeing around me was unbelievable. Even the orderlies were all "wide-eyed" and speaking softly around me. In a way, I appreciated everyone's respect but on the other hand, it seemed to make it more obvious that I was pathetic.

The labor did not begin for a long time but finally started about lunch time. Noah Benjamin then quickly arrived at 2:20 in the afternoon. Since we already knew he was a little boy and Mike had even named him a few months before, his arrival just happened quietly and without tons of emotion. I held my little guy in my arms and felt probably more alone than I had ever felt. It seemed so impossible to me to think about raising a new baby by myself.

A couple of hours later, my Dad arrived at the hospital with Mason Thomas. Mason was so excited about his new little brother and we all had a good time watching the two getting to know one another. In a few hours, everyone went home and I just lay alone in my bed holding my new little guy. Later in the evening, a young man came in to bring ice and I can still vividly remember the look on his face. He even had tears in his eyes as he filled my water jug, admired my new little guy and quickly scurried out the door.

My primary desire was to get home as quickly as possible so my Doctor granted my wish and let me leave the hospital early that next morning. On the way home that day, my Mom made a stop at the Social Security Administration office and I applied for Noah's Social Security card so he would be entitled to death benefits like his siblings. Filling out the paperwork that day in the lady's office was difficult to say the least. It also attracted lots of attention when people around us began to talk about my situation and the little guy with me who wasn't even 24 hours old. Once again, the thoughts came to me about how the "nitty gritty" life details still continue in spite of the circumstances you are in. I had no choice but to plow through situation after situation with composure and clarity. There is so much "fall-out" when someone dies, particularly when they are young like Mike.

Opening the Floodgates of Heaven

When I stop and really think about the condition I was in physically, emotionally, and financially when Mike died, it is almost overwhelming.

A little over two years before Mike's death, I was the Business and Economic Development Director for the Cherokee Tribe in Oklahoma. This was a high-level, high-stress sort of position. I enjoyed getting to exercise my MBA muscle and travel around the country but the position put a lot of stress on Mike. He was now in charge of taking the kids to school, picking them up, and starting all the after-school stuff like dinner and homework since I left before he did and arrived home an hour later than he. Well, to make a very long story much shorter, the Cherokee Tribe soon found itself (fall of 1995) in the midst of a nasty tribal election and "the other team" won – well, my position at the tribe was soon promised to someone else and I quickly resigned to come home and be a full-time mom. At the time of my resignation, Mason Thomas was quickly growing larger and larger in my tummy. Mason arrived on February 12, 1996.

So, on March 6, 1998, when Mike went on to be with the Lord, I had - soon to be - 4 children, no husband, no job, no income, probably about $300 in cash, and we had scraped together our last $14,000 in cash and had ALREADY paid that toward the 4 week cancer treatment program!

Mike and I had made some good decisions about money in our marriage and had a nice nest egg saved when he became ill. During the course of the 11 month illness, however, much of our money had been chewed up with the medical expenses. Yes, we did have good insurance but even good insurance doesn't pay 100% of the costs and just one of Mike's surgeries cost over $60,000.

It says in the Bible that our Heavenly Father is the Father to the Fatherless and the Defender of the widow and I just clung to that verse with all my might. Well my friends, I'm here to tell you LOUD and CLEAR that my God is certainly able to more than care for a widow and her babes in the most amazing way.

Like I said before, upon arriving home I learned our small hometown had already established a trust fund for our family and that people far and wide were pouring money into it. Our church, and neighboring churches we had once attended, joined the fund raising campaign. The entire Corps of Engineers system also began their own fund raising programs. Through these various avenues, our needs were met, and I did not have to feel one bit financially insecure. This was an immediate blessing. I could breathe and relax and begin to sort through all the confusing paperwork involved with life insurance, social security, insurance annuities, etc.

Other interesting stories began to unfold in the financial arena. First, through the course of normal life, I would receive bills, as we all do, to pay for things like car insurance, house insurance, electricity, etc. Well, after Mike died, I would sit down to pay a bill, write out the check exactly as requested, and low and behold many times I would receive either a refund for overpayment or would receive credit toward my next bill for overpayment. As this happened more than several times for me, I would even become amused wondering what new way God would find to provide abundantly for my family.

In another instance, I received a phone call from our Credit Union. The lady introduced herself and then began to explain to me that the Credit Union had a "special provision" for members who die between certain limited age ranges. She went on to say that if a member dies in that age range all current loans with them are immediately canceled! The Credit Union would also give a cash bonus back to the surviving spouse based on an average savings and checking balance during the past year. All I could think of was "wow," debt cancellation and a bonus check to boot! We only had one loan at the time and it was for a truck that we had just purchased, not a month before, for my 15 year old son.

I could actually fill a separate book with all the financial miracles and provision that resulted after Mike's death. I would, however, like to share a few more details. Within just a few weeks, I received news that since Mike died as a full-time employee, instead of being on disability my monthly survivor benefits (with my children's amounts included) would be about twice as much as expected. Funny thing to remember, but when we were scheduled to return home from Mexico after the 4 week stay, Mike would have been very close to needing to quit work or take medical disability since he had used all of his vacation and sick time and would have been completely out of leave time. Once again, God's strong hand of provision and protection had prevailed and our family had been spared this financial setback.

At about that same time, I was notified that Mike had paid enough quarters into Social Security to also draw those monthly benefits for the children and me. Because Mike had spent the last 20 years working for the Corps of Engineers in their Civil Service Program, he DID NOT pay Social Security out of his paycheck. Evidently though, during high school and college, he had miraculously paid in the proper amount of quarters and the children and I were soon receiving monthly SS benefits as well.

Soon, Mike's life insurance arrived and I then knew that my financial situation had "forever" changed. God had brought me from a penniless and jobless pregnant lady in a foreign country to a peaceful financial condition. I was so thankful!

New routines

Mike's passing brought so many significant changes in our daily life. At 5:00 p.m. every evening, he no longer came through that front door ready for dinner. At 10:30 at night, I no longer had someone to grab my arm and pull me up off the couch and head to bed. After supper in the evenings, the kids did not have a Dad who would head outside to play ball or go to the pond to just walk around and skip rocks. I no longer had someone to "tinker" with the lawn mower and keep it running, or change the oil or light bulbs. I no longer had a sounding board and best friend. In every aspect of our lives we had to develop new routines.

As described before, after Mike's death Jesus Christ truly became the Lord of my life. He was so real to me and I could just see and feel His hand all over my life. I ordered tons of Christian materials and would listen to tapes on every Biblical subject available, read new books, memorize entire chapters out of the Bible – I wanted anything and everything that was about God inside of me.

Recently in a church service, I heard the Pastor talking about what it means to "Walk in the Spirit." Galatians 5:16 says, "I say then: Walk in the Spirit, and you shall not fulfill the lust of the flesh – so as Christians we are commanded to walk in this manner." This verse is describing a process in a person's life where they consistently keep their soul (their mind, will and emotions) FULL of God. In this process, you constantly feed good information into your mind, will, and emotions so you are reacting and living life according to the Spirit and not the flesh. Our souls are constantly being filled with something all during our day, so a purposeful filling of oneself with God is necessary to obey the commandment. Even without knowing what that phrase or process really meant at that time in my life, I had unconsciously moved into a phase where I was allowing God to fully manifest Himself in my soul. I was learning to "Walk in the Spirit" and it felt really good!

During this season in my life, I also went on a nutty decorating scheme in my home. I decided that I wanted Scripture on every space in my house where a person's eyes might fall. I placed Scripture in some form or another to catch both eye and heart throughout my home. I wanted to receive inspiration through Scripture at a glance while in the recliner or in bed, while standing at the sink and sitting at the dining room table. The result was beautiful and inspiring, I think.

I learned so much during this process both about God and about myself. I had prayers answered mightily time and time again and I could hear God directing my actions. There were many times that He would have me do something very specific for people around me (sometimes the desire was directed toward people I hardly even knew) and I would be faithful to obey. This was the early beginning of my having true confidence that God would diligently direct my steps if I was just faithful to listen and obey. It was also the beginning of discovering my intercessory nature, which I did not fully understand until just recently. By intercessory nature I mean that God lays on my heart an intense concern and desire to pray for situations and people around me, and often He also directs me to reach out to specific people and allow Him to work in their lives.

However, part of what I was learning left me feeling like there was more information that was available – like I was only getting "part of the story" through my current church and their doctrine. It was hard to put my finger on at that moment in my life, but I remember many times feeling like I needed more.

Two years before Mike's death, when I had resigned from full-time employment, we had made the decision to try home-schooling our oldest son and daughter. This was an interesting experience and something that had worked out well for our family. Our routine was that I handled Emily's schoolwork and cared for Mason and the home and that Mike would work and manage Tyler's schoolwork after hours. Our decision to home-school had raised many eyebrows in our family and community but no one could argue that we weren't doing an effective job teaching our children.

I have great memories of this time in our life. Such as making a deal with Emily about her 3rd grade math that if she would memorize all of her multiplication facts I would take her to Red Lobster, just she and I, for a celebration lunch and I would allow her to order anything she wanted. Emily always had eyes bigger than her tummy and she always wanted to order adult food instead of off the kid menu, especially if it was a nicer restaurant. So, this little determined girl worked very hard and a few weeks later she was an official multiplication whiz! She and I then loaded into the car and headed to Red Lobster. At the restaurant I explained to the waitress about our "deal" and the waitress really went out of her way to make Emily feel special. Emily ordered shrimp cocktail for an appetizer, crab legs, and a fancy strawberry drink. It was so much fun to see her beaming with delight as we celebrated her big accomplishment. I'm sure she still remembers that day – I know I always will.

During our home-school time, Mike had been placed in a leadership program through his career and he often traveled to other states for classes. Because we were teaching our children at home, the children and I were able to accompany Mike on these adventures and we have great memories of field trips and times with Dad touring places like the Space Museum and summer camp in Huntsville, Alabama.

This home-school season in our life also prompted strong opinions from people in our life. I will never forget going to church on the Sunday after Mike's funeral. I should have stayed home but I was just driven to make sure my children were in church (thinking Mike would have wanted us to be drawn to the church and fellow believers during this difficult time.) Well, being a small church we all knew one another's business pretty much and there were a couple of people who were famous for sticking their noises into situations that maybe they shouldn't be in. One lady in particular approached me that Sunday in March, hugged my neck, and immediately said, "Guess now you'll have to put your kids back in public school." Her comment just cut me to the bone and I then made a decision that come hell or high water I was NEVER going to stop home-schooling.

It was obviously a bad mistake to make a decision like that based on anger and pride.

It wasn't until over a year later that I came to the conclusion that I was not able to properly home-school my children alone. At that point in my grieving process, I was exhausted, not sleeping, caring for two small babies, trying to handle all the new "guy" responsibilities that come with a home and yard, and then trying to properly school an 11 and 16 year old. At the one year anniversary of Mike's death, I experienced some of my most "down" moments. There was just something about that time frame that had finally brought all those raw emotions back to me. Maybe, immediately after a crisis like that, God shields you emotionally for a time making it possible for you to survive without totally losing your mind. It seemed like this year marker was a time when I had lost that shield and I was very graphically living in a place that was lonely and full of sadness.

It was during this time that God laid it on my heart that my children would be better off in a structured environment and that He would show Himself powerful and protect them from the influences that would come from being in the world's educational system once more. God showed me that I was doing an admirable thing (home-schooling) for prideful and arrogant reasons and that I needed to swallow my pride and admit that I was not being effective. I must say that was a very humbling experience.

Also, in the fall of 1999, I went over to Tahlequah to have lunch with a dear friend of mine. During the course of our lunch, I became aware that the museum she worked for needed a part-time grant writer. Through the course of several conversations (and especially since my children were back in school) I accepted the offer to work two days a week and write grants for this struggling organization. This much-needed mental exercise was a blessing to me and not long after the first of the year rolled around, I was working full-time as the Development Officer for this nonprofit organization.

God did amazing things through me in that position. It seemed as if everything that I wrote was funded. The organization only had eight employees when I first began in October 1999 and within 2 years they had about 38 full-time employees. The organization's annual visitation rose dramatically from around 41,000 to over 100,000 in about that same time frame. Over and over again, God just poured amazing financial provision out on this organization through the grants I would write.

Being employed full-time again and also being in the dating game somewhat meant this lady was pretty distracted. My days of spending all day reading my Bible, instructing my children, and listening to uplifting Bible teaching were gone. I quickly became pretty self-absorbed and in turn made some critical errors. I was no longer filling my soul (mind, will, and emotions) with things of God and instead, I was allowing the world to fill me. Errors come into our life when we begin to react and make decisions out of our flesh instead of our Spirit.

As I mentioned, I had begun to date during this season of my life and as I would spend time with person after person, I did not find what I was longing for. For some reason, I guess I expected that once I opened myself up for a new male relationship that an amazing man of God would just appear in my life, but obviously that just wasn't happening. I was growing more and more frustrated thinking that it was impossible for me to find love again. What I didn't realize at the time was that NO human person can fill that empty hole inside of another person. The only thing that would make me truly happy would be to allow my Savior, Jesus Christ, full control over my life.

I was also seeing the stress of my decisions affecting my children. In particular, my oldest son, who was a junior in high school at the time, was about to flunk out of school. He is a brilliant kid but was making some bad choices and I was too distracted to be much help. My little boys were tired and my daughter was involved with one friend in particular who was not a good Christian influence. I had also started gaining weight and was not exercising or taking proper care of myself.

A God-given Business

Tackling a big full-time job with 2 hours worth of commuting each day plus trying to date, manage a busy house, and raise 4 children wasn't a particularly HEALTHY idea for me. I was burning the candle at both ends and stress was starting to invade every waking minute of my time. As my one year employment anniversary rolled around, God was really dealing with me over my full-time job and lifestyle choices. Over and over in the course of a couple of months, God would wake me up in the middle of the night and place thoughts of RESIGNING on my heart, which I would quickly dismiss, not wanting to give up what I thought was a good deal for me.

However, there were lots of good things that came with my job. I was happier with my brain more active, the nice income was very welcome, and I really think my children were happier back in school. Even my little guys were enjoying their preschool and daycare even though the days got a little long for them.

After a couple months of waking up with the thought of resigning on my mind, I finally got up one morning at about 3:00 a.m. and typed out my resignation, giving two weeks notice. The next day I handed it in to the Executive Director who promptly told me that I couldn't do that and then proceeded to avoid talking any further to me during the next couple of weeks.

Toward the very end of my notice, the Executive Director of this nonprofit called me into her office to discuss the situation. She quickly told me that she would "do anything" to keep me writing grants for them, and for me to think about how this would work out. It felt nice being wanted or needed so badly, and I did enjoy writing. Thoughts of having a home-based grant writing business had actually been rolling around in my brain already so I began to firm up how I saw the arrangement materializing.

I then phoned a professional grant writer out of Oklahoma City whom I had met in a couple of professional organizations and I picked his brain as to how he structured his grant-writing contracts and what he typically charged for the service. Through these discussions, I was able to put together an agreement that would be a very profitable arrangement for me financially and would also greatly benefit this nonprofit organization as well – a win/win for everyone as I saw it.

I will never forget sitting down with the Executive Director to discuss my proposed contract. I would be responsible for all their grant writing and I had estimated that it would take me 20 hours per week to accomplish this task. I charged an hourly fee for that work and made that first contract effective for one year. The annual amount for the one year contract added up to just a little more than I was making as their full-time Development Officer. I thought, "*Hey! What will it hurt to ask for the moon and then negotiate down to something else?*"

As she read through the contract that morning, my heart was in my throat. I was wondering what she would say and how she would react. All at once, she grabbed her pen and signed it, then looked up and smiled and announced this was a great thing for both of us. We then spent a short time discussing logistics of how to flow the paperwork between the two places and my new job arrangement became a reality.

Once again, I was simply shocked at what God had done for me. I could almost hear God saying, "Duh, Rhonda, aren't you glad you finally decided to listen to me!" In just a matter of two weeks, I went from being so stressed trying to handle a big 40 plus hour job away from home to half the hours at home now for more money! God had proved himself mighty once again, or should I say, "Once He got my attention."

I quickly moved to incorporate the business so I could have tax advantages and retirement benefits offered through that type of legal arrangement. I made a trip to Office Depot for paperclips and copy paper, bought a fax machine, and I was set to successfully operate Clemons, Inc.

I loved working at home. I'm a disciplined lady so it wasn't much of a struggle most days to keep myself on track. If things with my children were on the agenda for the day, I would just sit up and work at night. This was just the ticket to keep my mind active, bring in a nice income, and give me the freedom to properly care for my home and family.

Not long after that first contract, other organizations heard I was now in this business and other contracts quickly came into my life. At one point about six months later, I had as much as 50 hours of contract writing a week. It was at this point in the process that I was probably busier than I ever was before, although it was easier because of being home based. I soon began to realize that satan is a good imitator of God's goodness. I really believe that during this stage of my business, satan was trying to give me TOO MUCH work so I would be distracted and ineffective in all that I was doing. After realizing that not every new work opportunity was straight from the hand of God, I began to scale down. Currently, I try to not exceed 25 hours each week. This gives me a nice flow of cash without the crazy lifestyle.

I've now had my own business since October 2001, and my income has continued to rise and remain stable. I am so blessed to have this financial soundness in my life, while at the same time having the freedom that comes with self-employment. Without God's mighty hand upon this area of my life, it would be much more difficult to handle the stress of several children and a career being a single Mom. There is just no other explanation for my successful business than believing and seeing that it came directly as a blessing from God Himself!

Fire!

In October 2001, I was sitting in my home office typing away on a grant and I received a phone call from my insurance company. The lady on the other end of the phone had several questions about my home. The purpose of the call was to make sure I had adequate homeowner's insurance coverage. I guess they just randomly picked policies to check on. As I look back on that phone call today, I laugh at myself for thinking this call was a random event. In reality, that phone call was straight from the hand of God. He was preparing to move my life in a better direction. I just didn't realize it at the time.

Because we had built our own home in several different intervals and had performed the majority of the work ourselves, it quickly became apparent to the insurance reviewer that our home was under-insured. She plugged all the information into a computer program and out popped a number, around $100,000, that was the magic number that it would cost to replace our home in today's dollars.

My policy was currently for only $50,000 and the annual premium was due the first part of December, just a few weeks away. I remember the lady from the insurance company on the phone asking me if I wanted to wait until it was time to pay my annual premium to "up" the amount of insurance I carried on my home or do it now. She cautioned me that if I made the amount effective on the date of the phone call, then I would immediately have to forward "X" amount of money to them for the difference. Before I even really thought about it, I said, "If that is what it would cost to replace my house, then I want that coverage – make it effective today and I'll place the extra money in the mail today."

On November 17, 2001, my Mother, daughter and I were all were going to go Christmas shopping in Ft. Smith. My Dad had offered to keep my two little boys at home and they all planned to have a "guys night out" and build a campfire and roast weenies and marshmallows in his pasture. Everyone had a nice time and I tucked my little warriors into bed that night chatting about their bon fire and how much fun they had with their Papa Tom.

The next morning was Sunday and after I had bathed and dressed myself and my little boys, the three of us all sat down together at the dining room table for breakfast. As they were finishing up, I excused myself and headed to my daughter's room at the other end of the house to finish drying my hair for church.

After just a few minutes and for no apparent reason I turned off the hair dryer and immediately could hear Noah and Mason rattling the doorknob in their room. Their bedroom door would stick really tightly and it quickly dawned on me that they had gone into their room after eating and had shut the door too hard and weren't able to get out now. About that time, I heard Emily leaving the shower which was next door to their bedroom so I yelled at her to open their door for them.

The next thing I heard was Emily screaming that the room was on fire. I ran up to the boy's room and the top bunk of their bunk bed was on fire. When the door was opened, Mason – the older of the two – quickly ran out of the room like a crazy man but little Noah was just standing there screaming his head off, frozen!

I tried to yell at Noah and tell him to run outside and get away from the fire so I could try to put it out but he wouldn't budge. I had to physically scoot him down the hall and after a quick swat on the pants, I ordered him to run out into the yard and get on the trampoline with his older brother.

Emily and I quickly began to run water in pitchers and pour on the fire. We tried to find the fire extinguisher but couldn't. I ran down the hall to my room and gathered my purse and tried to wake my oldest son Tyler who was sleeping in the room right by the fire – SOUND ASLEEP still!

Pretty soon, the whole room was engulfed with fire. It had just been a few minutes but it was already leaping through the roof. Emily, Tyler, and I all ran out of the house to join my little boys in the yard. Neither Emily nor Tyler even had time to grab any clothes. Thank God, I had a blanket in the back of my van (which I had just barely got out of the garage), so I was able to wrap that around Emily.

My parents, the fire department, and tons of neighbors rushed to the scene. It was an amazing thing to see my home burning to the ground and realize that I was totally helpless. I just kept thinking how close Mason and Noah had come to being killed in that burning room, probably minutes from death with that door stuck shut.

To this day, no one is really sure how the fire started. The prevalent theories are that somehow the boys saved some matches from the bon fire the night before and proceeded to recreate the camping scene on the top bunk of their bed. They also both said they cooked something in the oven and microwave that subsequently caught fire when they carried that into their room. That one is harder to believe because I had just been with them in the kitchen. Whatever the reason, my little 3 and 5 year old had created quite the problem.

As I explained earlier, Mike and I (along with other family members) had pretty much built our home ourselves. We started out in a tiny 640 square feet place that we built about a year after we married in 1981. Right before Emily arrived in 1987, we added on another addition about that same square footage. Finally, we added on a third addition with about the same square footage five years later – this gave us 4 bedrooms and around 2,000 square feet. After Mike's death, I completed the construction process by building a big attached garage and another bathroom. The end result of all this activity was a large home with no debt. Praise God!

The house was a tremendous financial blessing to my family but it also held millions of memories of my life with Mike. There wasn't an inch of that house that didn't remind me of something to do with Mike. I had several friends always tell me that they believed part of what made it so difficult for me to completely heal from his death was the house, filled with stuff all around me that just screamed Michael Clemons.

The house was also built on 2 acres that was given by my parents to Mike and me when we married. The 2 acres were connected to a much larger tract of land where my parents' home was located. My parents were not in favor of me ever selling the house and land because they didn't want people outside our family living so close to them. You see, living in the country around here are families on large tracts of land, and nobody is into the close neighbor thing unless maybe it's their own child.

I had my home up for sale at one time after I went to work full-time at the museum in Tahlequah. I was spending 2 hours a day driving to and from work. The house with all its memories was depressing me and I wanted a change. It wasn't long after this that a great girl's basketball coach moved into the Warner School System and my love for basketball prompted me to keep Emily in the Warner School System. I took my house off the market and stayed put. My parents were obviously relieved; selling the house would have probably caused a tremendous amount of friction between us.

As we were watching the house burn, my mother took my little boys and Emily to her home. The EMS people wanted to do a thorough evaluation on them and make sure no one was suffering any ill effects from the smoke. Emily was in the hand-bell choir at church and they were supposed to perform at 11:00 that Sunday morning. She insisted that she should still be allowed to go so she wouldn't let the group down. A nearby neighbor went to her home and gathered some jeans, a sweatshirt, and a pair of shoes which Emily quickly put on and wore to church. Little Noah Benjamin, then 3, was also hollering about not wanting to miss church so the neighbor took him that morning as well. That Sunday there wasn't a dry eye in that Baptist church as they watched my determined little girl play in the choir, wearing a mismatched outfit, while the fire department and her Mother were still in the yard watching their house burn.

That afternoon, a friend and I went shopping in Muskogee to gather the basics needed by our family. Where do you start, I thought. How in the world can you ever replace EVERYTHING? We gathered 3 outfits for each family member, shoes, toothbrushes, hairbrushes, backpacks, and other personal items – it was an amazing process to think of everything a person uses each day.

A friend from our church called that afternoon and said she knew of a family that had moved in with their elderly mother and father and had an entirely furnished house for rent. Did you catch that – <u>completely furnished</u> – they had just picked up their clothes and left to live elsewhere.

I phoned the lady and we made an appointment to meet that next Monday morning to discuss the specifics. I also talked with my insurance agent and made an appointment to meet with him on that Monday as well. The insurance guy assured me that my coverage was good and all would work out to our benefit – getting what we needed for immediate survival, getting us into another home, and replacing what we had lost. I felt much better.

On Sunday night, the children and I stayed with my parents. They were so kind to us. But I had tremendous trouble sleeping that night, as I just kept thinking about how close my little boys had come to being killed.

Monday rolled around and I was off and running handling all the millions of details that are included in replacing your home and all your belongings. I met with the lady about the house and was so amazed when I walked in to take a look at it. The home had everything still in place – you couldn't tell that someone wasn't living there. As I said before, they had just taken their clothing and moved in with her mother. It didn't take me long to say, "YES, we'll take it." I wrote her a check and she handed me the key.

In a matter of a little over 24 hours, God had already provided me a place to call home with all the bells and whistles. I would not have to worry about replacing any of the household items right away. All I had to do was get our personal things gathered and work out the insurance details so we could build or buy another permanent home.

Next, I went to the insurance office and we talked about the details of the policy. Because I had "upped" the policy amount a few weeks earlier and had even paid the new premium amount, I would receive approximately twice as much in coverage benefits than I would have otherwise. The company immediately wrote me a $3,000 check to pay for deposits, rent, buying new clothes and personal items, and for living expenses while we were out of pocket waiting to build or buy a new permanent house.

God is so good! As I lay in bed that night in the rented house, I could see the blessings starting to emerge from the situation. I could see that this was a God-led ordeal because of how mightily He was moving on our behalf. I love the Scripture that says how God will keep those <u>in</u>

PERFECT PEACE whose mind is stayed on Him. I could feel that peace in my life because I was trying very hard to keep my mind on God and not on the circumstances around me. I had learned through the process of losing Mike that if I would keep my focus on HIM, then all else would work out. I could handle the situation and have a confidence and peace in my life that is beyond understanding. Unless a person has been through a horrible tragedy in their life and experienced the peace that can come only from God, that person will probably have a hard time understanding my words here.

Even at this early hour in the fire phase of my life, I was already seeing how all the details connected with the fire just seemed to have already been worked out ahead of time to bless us through this situation. I knew the fire had a purpose and that part of that purpose was to teach us just how much God loves us and works ALL THINGS out to the benefit of those who love God and are called according to His purpose.

Dealing with the insurance company proved to be quite the hassle. They investigated the fire and concluded that it was an accident and began to assess and determine just how much of the policy would be paid out. The house did not completely burn to the ground. The middle part was completely destroyed and the two end sections of the house were still standing but horribly smoke and water damaged. Because it wasn't a clean cut "100 % destroyed" fire situation, negotiation was in order.

One of the first things that had to be done was to perform a complete inventory of every item we owned – room to room. Gosh, that was a chore. Thankfully though, my family pitched in and helped me inventory the items. As we sifted through the mess, it soon became apparent that all the replaceable stuff was pretty much totally lost and all the irreplaceable items (like baby books, wedding book, pictures, things of Mike's that were stored) were about 95% "OK." That was an amazing thing to me. I had stored these memories in plastic Tupperware-type boxes in my closet and this was the section of the house that was the least affected by the fire, smoke, and water. Once again, God showed Himself powerful. He allowed me to save those things that would have crushed my heart to have done without, especially the items connected with Mike. Then he provided the money that I needed to replace all the other extras that the children and I wanted and needed.

Within about a month and a half, I had the full insurance settlement in my hand. God had worked on my behalf and had given me the determination and ammunition I needed to persuade the insurance company to pay out at the maximum policy limit. Those of you who have dealt with professional insurance adjustors before understand how much of a miracle this actually was!

Also, during this process I had diligently been looking for another house. I had purchased building plan books but the thought of living in the small rental house and building a new permanent house seemed like more than I wanted to handle. One day in the evening, kind of late, I saw a real estate sign that I hadn't noticed in a while. I drove to the house and it was a big, beautiful two-story home on about 3 acres right by the city limits in Warner. I called about it, went to look at it, and immediately fell in love with the place.

The couple accepted my offer after a series of back and forth negotiations and I was off and running remodeling my new home. This was a fun ordeal and I say ordeal because it involved a TON of details. Remember now that I am a single mom to 4 active children with a big home-based business. Needless to say, I didn't get a lot of sleep during those few months of on-going renovations.

We signed the papers and moved into the new house on New Year's Eve with the construction still ongoing. I just laid in my bed in our new home that first night in amazement thinking of how powerfully God's hand had moved in the FIRE situation. I was now out of a house that was filled with painful memories and that I would never had been able to sell without displeasing my parents. I had been able to save all the irreplaceable things that meant so much to me, and God had miraculously worked out the details on the insurance policy to bring twice as much money into my hands for purchasing (paying cash, might I add) a wonderful new home which placed me close to the kid's school, without having to drive down miles of dirt road. God had once again shown me how much He wants to help me, how He is truly is the defender of the widow and the Father to the fatherless. He loved me and my family so much. He had blessed me and my family and had moved in our favor, BIG TIME, yet again.

A Fresh Perspective

Oh, just to back track a little bit… One day while in a nearby town shopping, I had stopped to have lunch at Sonic. While sitting there eating I noticed a construction sign across the road that read "For HIM Construction" with the Christian symbol of the fish on it. This greatly interested me so I wrote down the number for future reference.

Right before the fire occurred, I had called this gentleman to get some quotes on building some small single family apartment homes. I had a bit of an entrepreneurial streak in me and this seemed like a viable financial venture for our little college town with limited housing. Rodney Rogers pulled up that day and I immediately felt a familiarity about him – He was obviously a committed Christian and I was looking forward to possibly doing business with him and his construction company.

Rodney gathered all the details about the apartments and we sat down to talk about the process. We scheduled time for that Friday to firm up the deal and sign the contract. This was the Friday before my home burned on that Sunday. Well, for whatever reason Rodney and I did not connect on that Friday, but we spoke on that following Monday and I told him about the fire and my inability now to go forward with building the apartments. We both agreed that God was moving mightily on behalf of my children and me and that we would be fine, even better than before. He offered his remodeling services if I found a home that needed that sort of thing and I agreed to give him a call.

Well, I called Rodney as soon as I decided to purchase this new home. The house was very solid with good construction but it seemed so 1970s through and through. I set out to bring the house into at least the 90s and for a period of several months I was around Rodney almost on a daily basis. Since I work from home, I was there during the daytime when he and his crew were working on the house.

Rodney has one of the freshest perspectives I've ever seen in a Christian. He was not judgmental nor did he think he had it all figured out. He had a sincere desire to know more about God every day and he was always aware of opportunities around him that God had placed there for him.

Rodney truly understood what it was to "walk with God," to be spirit-led and spirit filled, and he practiced and lived what he knew was the "right" thing to do.

He was so interesting to me and I just couldn't get enough of "God" discussions with him. Because of the faith I had been raised in, there were several areas in the Bible that I had questions about that were never taught or practiced. Rodney had a way of explaining many of these issues that made sense. I always wondered why a Christian church could pick and choose around some of the very obvious things in the Bible.

Little by little, this fresh perspective of Rodney's began to make me yearn to be in a church where more of God's word was taught. Through Rodney living so FULL of GOD, I was now more open-minded, able to believe that this 'ole Christian lady might actually NOT KNOW everything, that there may be an even more abundant walk than I ever realized. I did not want to jump off into a bizarre and nutty experience but I did want to learn how to be a more effective disciple of Christ, how to live a more spirit-filled and victorious life.

At that same time the Baptist church I was attending was full of strife. It was an amazing process to watch, but for a very long time I was keenly aware that this Pastor was not listening to or following the God I knew so well. I wanted OUT but didn't know where to go.

In February 2001, one of my business contracts offered me the opportunity to travel to Washington, D.C., with one of their full-time employees for a conference specifically related to one of the funded grants I had written for them. Eleanor was the Office Manager for this organization and she and I met at the airport in Tulsa for a five-day trip to our nation's capital.

I will never forget that Eleanor was reading a book called "Avoiding Deception" (obviously a Christian-themed book) when I walked up to her in the airport. She had a big sweet smile and was just the type of person anyone could see was filled with the Spirit of God. It didn't take long for us to hit on the subject of our churches.

During that week together, I would mention something about my church that I was frustrated with and she would always come back with something like this: "At

Cornerstone, Pastor Allen teaches so and so. I applied that principal and it just really impacted my life and family in a positive way. He is so open, and funny, and he really loves and cares for people in the church." By the time I arrived back home from the trip, I got off that airplane vowing that I was going to attend Cornerstone Church no matter how far a drive it might be.

So, around the middle of February on a beautiful Sunday morning, I gathered my children and we made an hour's drive to Cornerstone Fellowship Church in Tahlequah, Oklahoma. Cornerstone was a non-denominational church and I had no idea what to expect. Cautiously we walked in the door and were met by several friendly faces, including Eleanor's. She was so surprised that we had come. Pleasantly surprised, I might add.

Well, the music started and this girl immediately realized she wasn't in Kansas anymore... Everyone was on their feet, the music was jazzy and loud, and pretty much everyone was clapping their hands and really enjoying the worship time. My daughter and I just stood there frozen, looking around in amazement. I had never seen people REALLY enjoying music in church – ever!

I will also never forget this one particular lady who captured my attention that first day. She was sitting in the middle section of seats on the outside. Before church started (we were early that morning – I'm almost always early!) I watched her as she made her way around the entire building just shaking hands and hugging people. She had such a sincere expression and seemed to just ooze "God" if you know what I mean. During the praise and worship time there that first day at Cornerstone, this little blond lady was about to explode. You could tell, she worshipped with her hands held high to God, singing from the bottom of her heart. I was amazed.

The message that first Sunday was a wonderful teaching, the beginning of a new series called "How to find the right mate." Through this series, the Pastor was not only trying to teach people how to be attracted to the right kind of person, he was using the Fruits of the Spirit to instruct every person there how to live more victoriously and how to develop these essential characteristics in each and every heart.

This was just the kind of practical, God-filled information that I wanted to hear. I had sat in a church/ denomination all my life that preached 95% salvation messages and I always thought, "I'VE DONE THAT ALREADY – at least 30 years ago! – I want to be discipled. I want to know how to have that joy that I had seen in Rodney, Eleanor, and that little blond lady I saw that first day at Cornerstone." I had sat in a church or denomination that talked about the problem, but not much more. In fact, they were really good at going over and over what the problems were in life but they never gave the practical answer on how to GET OUT of the problem... but this church did. I was hooked!

Every Sunday and Wednesday after that, I was there in that same seat with my notebook in hand, furiously writing down all the things he was saying. I had grown accustomed to the great music and enthusiasm in the praise and worship time and had even started clapping my hands. I know you are probably laughing thinking about someone being so "uptight" in their worship time that they can't even clap without feeling it was wrong but that was where I was in my thinking. I knew the church believed in the spiritual gifts from talking with Eleanor but NEVER did I see anyone do something "odd" like scream, run around, or fall down. You know, the things you always imagine that Charismatic churches might do?!?

After a few months, I had gathered quite a list of questions based on things the Pastor had taught that didn't line up with what I had always learned. I outlined these things in a very coherent format along with Scriptures that "I thought" made my point and I called the church office to request a meeting with the Pastor. Rosita answered the phone and she was very pleased to schedule some time with the Pastor that following Wednesday to talk about my thoughts.

I walked into Pastor Allen's office that Wednesday ready to discuss things, excited that he was taking the time to listen to me and present his "take" on my questions. One by one, we took the questions and through three Bibles and an on-line Bible program in the original languages of Greek and Hebrew we sorted through the Scripture and found the answers.

On some of the issues, I had been completely ignorant of what the verse meant in the original language. On other questions, I was simply wrong and I was "right on" a couple of times as well. It was an enlightening experience that opened my eyes to the fact that I needed to not just "swallow" what someone was teaching me but needed to dig in and find out what the verse was really saying.

Pastor Allen soon began to realize that I was "chock-full" of Calvinistic philosophy and he recommended that I listen to and study a long tape series on this exact doctrine, which I promptly did. Listening to that information and realizing that many of my thought processes toward God were based on this "theory" instead of what Scripture taught was eye-opening and life changing.

Later that summer, I officially joined Cornerstone and I've never looked back. Sitting under such anointed teaching and applying the principals I was being taught has made all the difference.

Dying to self – Climbing upward one more step…

After finding Cornerstone, my life began to change for the better. I was beginning to have a deeper fellowship with God and was making some wonderful new friends. Things just seemed to be rocking along quite nicely for me and my family.

Seems to me like when I begin to really feel comfortable in a situation – maybe not learning and growing anymore – that's when satan will try to sneak in and do his trick of stealing, killing, and destroying things in my life.

If a person had asked me in this period of my life how things were, I would have said, "Wonderful but…" It wouldn't have taken me very long to tell them that I felt all was well in my life and with my walk with God, except I wanted another mate who would be a good role model for my children. It was like deep down in my subconscious, I truly believed that I couldn't be complete without this piece fulfilled – that our family was incomplete and lacking in this area. It's difficult to say but I guess that what I really was saying was that God, by Himself, was not enough for me!

It was because of this reason that I did not totally let God have the reins in life. I hadn't yet laid it ALL DOWN at his feet. I now truly believe that every person has to come to this crossroad if they are to continue to mature in Christ. A person may lay down one issue after another but until you Totally Die to Self, lay it all down at His feet and surrender your life completely, without strings, into your heavenly Father's hand, then you will not climb to that higher level of fellowship with the Almighty. Until then, He will not truly be the Lord of your life.

In February 2003, I was standing at this very crossroad making my decision whether I would die to self or turn and walk the other direction away from God. Between February 2003 and Good Friday right before Easter, I wrestled with this issue.

In the course of my busy life, I had met a gentleman through my work, an amazing Christian man who was so full of energy and life. He had a wonderful way with people, especially children. Through our working relationship, we became very good friends and I learned many things about him, all of which impressed me greatly.

It soon became apparent that he and I thought very much alike. We truly enjoyed one another's company and our relationship continued on for several months. One morning early in the beginning of 2003, I dreamed of this person and when I awoke that next day, I knew I was in love. It just hit me like a ton of bricks. I hadn't let myself think like this at all – it never was my intention – not for one single minute because you see… this person was married.

Things moved pretty fast from that point on – our relationship kept progressing and we soon came to the point where we talked about what was happening. By saying it "out-loud" things became much different. Before it was easy to just assume that these thoughts weren't real or dangerous because a lot of the time what was happening could be easily explained away. We were never physical or inappropriate in a sexual sort of way. But that didn't mean there wasn't a serious problem.

After we both knew how we felt, we eventually agreed that this was a dangerous game to be playing and I asked that he not contact me anymore. I needed to be away from him and get him out of my mind. All was well with my new resolve to get away from this man, but only for about 3 days. After that, he suggested that we could just "be friends." We could still talk and give one another insight and direction but not be in the mode of trying to be a couple. Like a fool, I fell back into the game.

Well, things once again started heating up and my heart continually felt like it would explode. I would give him HUGE amounts of my time and energy but I could never actually "be" with him. This was a great deal for him because he could have his cake and eat it too. He could pick my brain, gather my support and admiration on all issues in his life; laugh and talk with me, and then go home to his wife. I don't think that even today he sees anything wrong with what was going on, since it wasn't physical and we had decided earlier not to pursue divorce. This whole ordeal was just fun to him. Talk about being deceived...

On my end though, this was NOT a good plan. I crawled into my cold bed every night alone after feeding him almost every available second of my extra energy and time during the day. I was slowly dying. I was miserable. I had let my relationship with God and my children take a serious back burner in my life, and I knew what decision I had to make but I just couldn't quite give this up. <u>He seemed perfect to me in so many ways – just what I thought I truly wanted out of life for both myself and my children.</u>

Although on the outside I was still handling life, on the inside I just kept falling further and further away from where I wanted to be with God. I couldn't effectively pray or read my Bible, and the longer this continued the more miserable I became. I was horrible and grouchy with my children and I knew that I had to make a decision to either stay with him and wait until one day when he would be free from his wife or cut him loose completely.

On the Thursday night before Good Friday, I finally snapped. It was just a combination of many things but that night I made the decision to get away from this person – to NOT play the game anymore. No more contact. I laid it down and agreed to play the game God's way, and if that meant losing the person who I thought would make me happy someday then I would just have to lose him. I had to be obedient.

That Friday morning I awoke with more peace in my heart and I was able to pray but I also had panic rising in my throat. I just knew that he wouldn't honor my request to stay away (why should he this time, he hadn't done it before) so I immediately started trying to call my friend Eleanor who now worked with our church on a part-time basis. My immediate thought was that I needed to get people praying for this guy to leave me alone. I wasn't sure if he continued to contact me whether I would be able to keep from getting sucked into the situation again.

Finally, I reached Eleanor and I quickly took off to have lunch with her in Tahlequah. I needed desperately to gather strength and receive prayer from people who wanted me to make the right decision. After lunch, I also met with my Pastor's wife and she spent a long time talking through the critical nature of this circumstance and how I MUST stay out of this, warning me how it could destroy my life. I totally agreed. It felt like I was standing on the edge of a huge canyon ready to swallow me up.

I felt much stronger after spending the day with supportive people and I drove home with peace starting to flood my heart and soul. I knew it would be a difficult process to get this person out of my heart and head, but I just knew that with God's help, I would be successful.

Later that next week, I had lunch with a wonderful lady, Norma Rice, who my friend Eleanor had suggested several times that I meet. Norma had been widowed a year before me and she was an awesome leader in our church. She was that little blond lady who had caught my eye the first day I had attended Cornerstone. She was full of God, on fire to serve Him with every fiber of her being.

Norma and I had a good visit and she really encouraged me in my decision to get out of this tricky relationship. She shared with me several of her life stories that involved bad decisions, which made me feel much better. I felt like such a spiritual failure to have made the big mistake that I had made but, looking at her and her walk with God and now knowing she had also made some critical errors in life, it was comforting to me. It made me feel like I had hope of being able to be used by God in a mighty way or to find deep and abiding fellowship with God again.

During the course of the lunch, Norma mentioned her prayer language. She said that when she received the baptism of the Holy Spirit it made a huge impact on her life. Although this was only briefly mentioned, it caught my attention. Since I hadn't seen anyone in Cornerstone practicing this gift, I was filled with questions about how and why. What was prayer language all about?

Norma also told me how her present powerful walk with God had begun. She took a season of time away from her normal life and dedicated every second to learning and growing in God – through music, Scripture, writing, reading – anything to get God into her head and heart. I had experienced something similar after losing Mike and I decided to now give it another shot… to have another love affair with the best guy, Jesus Christ!

Almost immediately following my decision to lay down this relationship, God impressed me to deal with two different issues which at the time seemed very strange and unrelated: 1) learn about the gift of tongues and 2) find my ministry, stop being so selfish and start being a Christian asset.

I had never heard our Pastor preach about the gift of tongues nor had I noticed anyone using this gift in the church but I had seen the tape series listed in the church tape catalog. I quickly ordered the set to figure out why God had placed this desire so strongly within my heart.

A New and Beautiful Language

Depending upon your spiritual or church background, you may feel uneasy at this juncture in the book. I know for myself, just the mention of the word "tongues" always produced an anxious and uncertain feeling in me during most of my Christian walk. I was raised in a denomination that believed this gift no longer existed. The only other thoughts I had about this gift was what I "imagined" happened at charismatic churches. I had a mental picture of people screaming, rolling around on the floor, being totally ridiculous and out of control – certainly acting in a way that would never receive God's approval. If you currently think in this way, please know that I was once right where you are. I sat in church 3 times a week, reading my Bible, praying, and only realizing a fraction of the power God has made available to every believer. Please be patient and open minded as you read through my journey of coming to understand and embrace this gift from God.

As I listened to the tape series by my Pastor about this subject, I was immediately amazed at how much I DID NOT know about the Baptism of the Holy Spirit and tongues. He used one Scripture after another to explain the doctrinal position of the Baptism of the Holy Spirit. I learned that tongues is simply prayer and is listed in 1 Corinthians 12:10 in the list of the nine manifestation gifts given by the Holy Spirit... the Holy Spirit distributes these gifts to individuals as He wills.

I learned that tongues is defined as the supernatural manifestation of the Holy Spirit by which the Holy Spirit speaks through us in a language that we do not know and do not understand.

The Pastor used many Scripture references to show not only that the Baptism of the Holy Spirit is real, but that it is received subsequent to our salvation. There are many Scripture references to show this, one being the story of Saul's conversion on the road to Damascus. In these verses in the 9th chapter of Acts, Saul's conversion experience is relayed. In verse 6 Saul calls Jesus "Lord." In his letter to the church at Rome, Paul taught that this declaration provides salvation which means that the Holy Spirit was now living inside Saul.

Later in those verses we read about God's instructions to Ananias to seek out this man named Saul who has had a vision and is waiting for him on a particular street. In verse 17 the NKJV says: "And Ananias went his way and entered the house; and laying his hands on him he said, 'Brother Saul, the Lord Jesus, who appeared to you on the road as you came, has sent me that you may receive your sight and be filled with the Holy Spirit.'"

When a person accepts Jesus Christ as their Lord and Savior, the Holy Spirit immediately comes to dwell in them. However, God intended for us to also "be filled", to receive the "Baptism of the Holy Spirit." When a believer receives this second baptism he is "endowed with power from on high", filled to overflowing with the attributes (characteristics) of the Holy Spirit. This believer will experience His power and indwelling in such a tremendous way that it impacts his entire life. Luke 24:49 says – "Behold, I send the Promise of My Father upon you; but tarry in the city of Jerusalem until you are endowed with power from on high."

The Baptism of the Holy Spirit is not necessary for salvation and is not forced on any believer. Although people can live their entire lives without experiencing this baptism, after hearing the reasons for this baptism and the change it brings into a believer's life, I was convinced pretty quickly that I wanted this gift.

The tape series also taught that because God is Spirit and we are flesh communicating between the two is sometimes very difficult. Romans 8:26 (NKJV) says, "Likewise the Spirit also helps in our weaknesses. For we do not know what we should pray for as we ought, but the Spirit Himself makes intercession for us with groanings which cannot be uttered." The word "with" does not appear in the original Greek. Because of the grammatical structure a better translation would be the Holy Spirit makes intercession for "our" groanings. This simple grammatical correction makes a great difference in how this verse reads.

It has become obvious to me that the point of Romans 8:26 is we as fleshly people do not know how to pray as we should. When we are faced with this situation, the Holy Spirit can make intercession to our Father for us (through tongues in our prayer language). This can happen in situations where we are so frustrated that we don't even have the words to describe our emotions.

Another interesting part of this verse explained on the tape series was the word "weaknesses". In the original language weaknesses is actually referring to one common weakness (singular in form – not plural) known to all mankind – one very specific weakness. The meaning is that we as humans DO NOT know how to pray as we should; we don't have the proper revelation knowledge, so we don't know what is best in many of life's circumstances.

The Pastor went on to explain that for God to answer a prayer two conditions must be satisfied. We must ask and we must ask according to God's will. John Wesley once said, "God does nothing but by prayer." Because we live in a sinful world and God has given us free choice, there can be circumstances going on which God would like to intervene in and change but unless He is asked for the answer to the situation according to His perfect will, the change will not occur. James 4:3 (NKJV) says – "You ask and do not receive, because you ask amiss, that you may spend it on your pleasures."

Working through this process in a very logical, scripturally based way, I've come to the following conclusions: 1) We as humans have a common weakness which is that we do not know how to pray as we should 2) One job of the Holy Spirit is to make intercession for us, through our prayer language, for our problems in life – our groaning 3) We can become so frustrated with these problems we don't even have words to express our need 4) "God does nothing but by prayer." But, for a prayer to be answered, we must ask God and ask according to His perfect will.

Based on these conclusions, I quickly came to the realization that powerful answers to prayer can occur in believer's lives when they have the Baptism of the Holy Spirit and experience their own private prayer language.

I also realized that praying in tongues was not the weird and mystical experience that I once thought. Receiving the Baptism of the Holy Spirit, which is how one would experience tongues, is a very real event that is subsequent to salvation and also well documented in the Bible. I was amazed that this information had always been in front of me, yet I had not been in a teaching environment where this truth was revealed.

Accepting the Baptism of the Holy Spirit doesn't have anything to do with salvation. A person can be a Christian and choose not to be obedient in this way, nor does it have anything to do with ones spiritual maturity. The Pastor gave several examples of very immature Christians who experienced and practiced the gift of tongues. Because tongues is a "Gift" it's given to believers wanting it, simply because God is good and wants to bless us, not because we have done "works" or grown to the point where we deserve it.

Pastor Allen explained that tongues have two places in our lives. One was in our own private prayer language and the other was in a corporate church sense. Private-time prayer language is the most common use of tongues and it enables a Christian to be used as a vessel for praying the perfect will of God into reality. He explained that Christians who open themselves up to this gift will experience a higher level of fellowship with God. <u>It brings a heightened sense of peace and greater clarity of thought into the Christian's life.</u> .

The second way tongues can be used is to edify or instruct the church body. I had never seen this practiced, but on occasion God will lead a person to speak in tongues in a church service and either that person or someone else would interpret the message. When talking about this type of circumstance, the Pastor was very careful to explain that most charismatic churches did not handle this properly. Everything should be done in a decent and orderly fashion, never in a way that would confuse or scare someone attending the church who did not understand what was happening.

This type of thinking was just what I needed to hear – realizing that the entire Bible is still relevant – that it is not necessary to pick and choose what you think still applies in your life, but knowing that God commands order, balance and self-control in all things.

Through this teaching, I learned that the Holy Spirit is a gentleman and that praying in the Spirit, either in church or in your own private prayer time, is completely and at all times under your control. There is never a circumstance where people should let themselves get too carried way – be disruptive and such... A believer with the gift of tongues is able to start and stop speaking in his prayer language at any time – always under his own discretion and control.

I also learned that tongues may be spoken in the languages of men or in angelic dialects but the one speaking does not understand the language at all. God will often give that person general knowledge about what he is praying for but the person speaking the tongue does not understand the language. This just sounded amazing to me.

Wow! I couldn't believe what I had heard when I completed all the tapes. I searched through the scripture references and prayed about what I had heard – it all settled perfectly within me – I had a total peace about the process. I had already sensed that some people in my life, like Rodney, Donna, and Norma were fellowshipping at a place that I did not quite understand or had not experienced. I knew there was more and now I understood what it was.

Based upon my new information, I sat out to "pick the brains" of some ladies in my church to whom I felt God had led me. As a part of this process I emailed two very precious Christian ladies (Donna and Norma) and began asking them questions. They were instrumental in helping me understand the "actual" process of obtaining tongues and they were (and still are) a great encouragement in my search to experience MORE of God each and every day.

The next day after listening to the tape series, I awoke in the morning with a song playing in my head that we sing at church. It has a line that says something like "Holy Spirit come – move in power…" and that verse played over and over in my head all day. I had moved from not understanding and actually looking upon tongues as something bad to now being ready to welcome this experience into my life.

That day as I walked early in the morning, I was really thinking about tongues – wanting to experience this gift – and talking to God about giving this to me. Not long into my walk; I began to hear a phrase in my head – obviously a phrase in a different language. I voiced that phrase and when I did, I just knew that was the beginning.

For five miles that morning, I walked and repeated that same phrase over and over again – I felt very excited

– sort of like I had adrenaline pumping throughout my body. I couldn't wait to get back home to email my "tongue coaches" and tell them that this experience was beginning for me.

During the course of the next few days, I would hear different phrases down inside myself and I would repeat those. Most of the time, these sounded like little rhymes – little sing songie verses. This was exciting for me but it felt like work – trying hard to hear something down inside myself and then repeating it back – so I asked more questions…

My friend Donna responded to my question about it seeming so difficult – trying to bring forth the tongue by hearing it first and then saying what I heard out-loud. Donna responded with a thought that changed how I was dealing with the situation. She told me that speaking in tongues is all about FAITH – That a person who totally desires this gift, just should open their mouth and begin speaking and out will flow the tongue – not your normal language. As I bathed that night after reading her email, I was convinced that was what I needed to do. Relax and believe – <u>just open my mouth in faith and it would flow.</u>

After my bath, I snuggled in my bed and began to pray. I told God that I now understood what the purpose of tongues was to a Christian. I told Him that if this was the way that the perfect will of God could be asked for and received in situations then I wanted this gift with every fiber of my being. I told God that He could use me in a mighty way to accomplish many things in His kingdom – that from now on I would just consider myself a vessel and I would allow the Holy Spirit to have total control over my life. I said that I totally believed He wanted to give me this gift and all I had to do now was just to open my mouth and speak and it would happen. I then stopped praying, took a deep breath, and began to speak – IN AN AMAZING AND DRAMATIC WAY!

The experience that followed was astounding! I found myself in a deep state of emotion, crying and even shouting, and I could just feel it pouring out of me. I was thinking in my natural mind that this was NOT WHAT THE PASTOR had described – This felt out of control and scary to me…The intenseness of this feeling was really surprising to me and after what only seemed a few minutes of speaking in tongues, I stopped myself. I looked at the clock and about 30 minutes had passed though it seemed like only a minute or two.

I immediately began to feel peace coming over me but I then let my imagination run wild. I was thinking, "Oh, great – I've asked for this thing to happen to me and now the next time I'm in church, I'm going to be rolling around and screaming just like I had imagined people speaking in tongues would act." This was NOT a comforting thought to me at the time.

I got up, got a drink, and tried to calm myself down. I didn't understand the intense emotions flowing out of me and I certainly didn't think I wanted to try that again. I sat down at the computer and typed an email both to Donna and Norma describing what just happened. After I got those thoughts down on paper, I went back to bed.

Once back under the covers and relaxing, God was just laying it on my heart to try it again - open myself back up and try it one more time. I finally thought, "Ok God – I'll give it another shot." I opened my mouth and in faith once again began to speak. All I could think then was "It's happening again – just like before!"

After what just seemed a few minutes of this crazy behavior, I stopped myself once again and upon looking at the clock realized the same thing had happened again – much more time had passed than I expected. I shot out of that bed and once again emailed my friends – begging for some explanation of what they thought this intense thing happening to me might be.

After going through the calming process once again, I returned to bed. This time I totally ignored anything God was saying – I had had enough fun for one night!

I awoke very early the next morning, and the first thing on my mind was all that had happened the night before. I lay there remembering what had happened and once again wondering what the purpose of tongues was in our life. I wanted in the worst way to think that my mouth was praying the perfect will of God into reality – I wanted to have sweeter fellowship, clarity of thought and the peace that I recognized in some of the people in my life. I prayed to God some, talking about these thoughts and once again telling Him that I would try it just ONE MORE TIME. I then opened my mouth and began to speak and out flowed the sweetest conversation you have ever heard. It sounded very much like an Asian dialect and it was fluid and totally peaceful. I lay there that morning hearing myself talking on and on – it was just like I was wrapped in a warm blanket and staring into a beautiful sunset or something. I had nothing on my mind except intently listening to these strange words flowing out of me.

After awhile, the tongues began to slow and then stopped. I was so excited! I jumped up and looked at the clock and to my total shock – I had lain there and prayed for over an hour! After finishing, I began to feel a peace that I still can't adequately describe. All day that day, anytime I wanted to, I just opened my mouth and out flowed the most amazing conversation over and over again.

About the same time that morning my friends Donna and Norma were both reading their "Oh My Gosh- what's happening to me!" emails. I soon received a response from Donna saying that she felt my first experience was some type of intercessory prayer – she comforted me saying not to be afraid and that I should praise God because

I might have just prayed an African missionary through some amazing life-threatening experience. When Norma responded later she had more concerns and suggested because I had gotten so frightened that I might need to meet with the Pastor and describe the situation – get his take on what happened. I immediately called Rosita at his office and she sat up an appointment for the following day – Wednesday at lunchtime.

I awoke early that Wednesday morning just praying away – even before my eyes were open – I just thought – "Gosh, I love this…" The day before, my grant writing and decision making had been so crisp. I'm normally a very sharp lady but things were different – I was experiencing the clarity of thought that so many people had described to me.

All the way to Tahlequah that Wednesday, I prayed in the Spirit. It was totally effortless and peaceful – it just flowed from me as if it had always been there – speaking in this new and beautiful language was as much a part of me as English.

I met my Pastor and his wife for lunch and we sat down and began to talk about my experience. He had a little sweet smile on his face as I described what had been happening to me the past few days. After listening to the story about the intenseness of last night, he assured me that it sounded like intercessory prayer and that God would only allow me to experience intense emotions like that in the privacy of my own prayer closet. He also said that my experience with prayer language was accelerated and that it was not usual for a person to have such an experience until much further in their walk.

He asked me if I had trouble stopping it when I started feeling uncomfortable and I said, "NO". I told him that I was totally in control of what was happening and had even stopped myself from trying the third time that night. When I didn't want it, it didn't happen again. He then described his first experience and assured me that being frightened of the intense anointing in the beginning is very normal.

After realizing that I was “OK”, we talked at length about not only how important this is to a Christian’s walk but also how important it was to understand its proper use. He asked me if I would have continued to attend and grow at Cornerstone Church, if the entire congregation was speaking in tongues the first time I went there. Now, I totally understood why God wants this gift to be used with maximum discretion and always decently and in order. If Cornerstone had run me off with improper behavior in the beginning, I would never have progressed to this stage in my understanding. I was so thankful my Pastor was wise and used God’s principles to operate his church.

I left Tahlequah that day on top of the world. I now understood the peace and fellowship people had described to me. This was probably the most amazing thing that had ever happened to me. I was so thankful!

Here are many of the actual emails that popped back and forth between Donna, Norma and I during this process:

Hey *again my new Tahlequah friend... (Donna)*

I enjoyed reading about how you received the gift of tongues and how that has comforted you in some of your darkest times. All day today (actually the first thing that was in my mind this morning) was that song we sing at Cornerstone - "Holy Spirit come - move in power...." That has played softly in my brain ALL DAY - maybe that means I'm relaxing more about this and accepting the idea...

I have some dumb questions and I'm just going to ask them anyway about this subject - I normally (almost never) pray out when I'm alone with God- I may very softly say the words but most of my prayer time leans toward silent to soft. Of course, I pray out in audible tones when I pray with my kids at night, dinnertime, etc. Do I need to be really voicing my prayers in a louder voice (where I can physically hear what I'm saying) when I'm alone. I walk almost every morning for exercise and I will pray as I walk but its more like a soft mumble - I'm not hearing what I'm saying - just knowing what I'm saying because its coming from within?? (I just read that and it sounds silly but isn't meant to be - does my question make sense?)

Norma described her prayer language to me - Norma told me that she will continually pray during church sometimes in tongues (quiet and under her breath while the Pastor is preaching and during the alter call)...

Which part of Tahlequah do you live in? My plan is to move to Tahlequah in 3 years when my daughter graduates high school. I desperately want to live in the same community in which I worship. I've looked in some areas and want to make a good decision. Please give me your Tahlequah housing area recommendations...

I need to bathe and tuck in my little warriors. I'll be in Tahlequah tomorrow again for a short meeting and to gather some information to put together a business plan for an organization.

Have a blessed evening and remember - it's easier on the hips to email Rhonda than to indulge in a Twinkie...Rhonda

Norma –

I listened to Pastor Allen's tapes yesterday and I now understand what tongues mean and how God uses them - I was totally ignorant before.

I was jarred out of sleep last night and prayed very long in the middle of the night - I felt it was close and this morning while I was walking, I was praying out loud and I received two or three phrases. My hands are still shaking now and I feel like how a person feels when Adrenalin pumps through them (or that's the best way to describe it right now) I just repeated those same phrases over and over again - for 5 miles - I didn't feel silly but peaceful - I'm looking forward to God fully developing my prayer language and I'm so looking forward to being able to pray the perfect will of God - there are so many areas of my life and with my children that honestly I don't know what is best so I'm unable to pray effectively I'm sure...Rhonda

Hi Norma,

From the couple of phrases that initial day, I've spoken three or four more times. There are different phrases and it sort of sounds sing-songie - like a song in a way instead of like talking or conversation. Is that normal? Also like I told you in church, one of the times I just kept having all these thoughts running through my head as I prayed - like maybe that was what I was praying about - I don't know??

Is it also normal to sort of hear the tongue down in yourself - like a tiny little noise and then open your mouth and voice that same thing you are hearing because that is sort of the way it started the first day. Or should it be me just opening my mouth and out coming something that I'm not feeling rising inside of me. Gosh, I hope that question just made sense??

It makes me feel so good that this blessing of tongues was right on the other side of my struggle to totally die to self. What a blessing to receive this after one of my largest struggles. If I hadn't surrendered that relationship then I would have lost out on this level of worship and victory - amazing stuff, huh? Rhonda

Rhonda Clemons

Hey Rhonda,

I think just being filled and not use to your prayer language that it can come in lots of ways. and may be in only one way for a while...I've heard of people singing in the spirit first, and I've heard of people just praying for an hour or more with a full language. I think it sounds wonderful in song....kind of rhyme like...anyway no set rules we're all different and I think receive different.....

I can speak in tongues just by opening my mouth and speaking knowing I am going to do that....the more I pray and really get involved the stronger it can become as I concentrate on prayer...sometimes it seems more inspirational and inspired and anointed and sometimes I am starting out in the flesh to allow my mind to be clear so I can clearing think about GOD and how I want to pray in my understanding about a subject....it clears your mind to get more in-tune to God's I think, and that takes starting in the flesh and letting the words come out of your mouth...not necessarily feeling like its deep within at first....does that make sense?.....I think sometimes I'm more inspired by GOD to pray so it comes really easy and powerful, other times its not much more than a few words.....I think you can always speak in tongues if you desire too...its by faith anyway...build your faith and keep praying.....just let God lead you and don't get discouraged...its a journey that's full of adventure and fulfillment.....there's nothing like the very first time though.....does that help?

Guess I should close and get ready for bed....We'll have to do lunch sometime....

Love ya, Donna

Hello Rhonda!

Sorry I haven't had the time to check my emails since Sunday early afternoon.

First I want to explain my comment Sunday (on the run). What I was trying to tell you when you said while you were praying in tongues thoughts were running through your head was that sometimes when you are praying in the Spirit the Lord gives you an interpretation of what you are praying. In other words an understanding in your natural mind. Perhaps that was what was happening. Then on the other hand, we sometimes wander off mentally on our own. That was the reason for my comment. What I was saying was to check yourself to see if the thoughts running through your head were "day dreaming" or if you believe they are God speaking to you.

Rhonda you seem to be getting frightened. I don't want that to happen. Fear is not what God wants for you either. I'm not sure I can address your last two emails without talking to you. All I can do is relate some of the times I have experienced what I describe as intense prayer in the Spirit. There have been a few times that I have been overcome with emotion...crying...and felt an urgency within me as I prayed. I did not know why nor did I know what I was praying about. I just know that the Holy Spirit knows and I trust Him and am happy to be a tool. I have not however, after I finished praying, felt ANY KIND OF DISCOMFORT OR FEAR. As a matter of fact I feel peaceful. I may not feel peaceful while I am praying in tongues but I always do afterward.

These times where I feel urgency and intenseness, I ask the Lord to give me understanding. Sometimes at church I feel like that. Most of the time, someone approaches me to pray for them, OR the Lord impresses upon me to go greet someone and ask them if I can pray for them about anything. Sometimes I have an understanding or Word of Knowledge about their situation without asking them.

Other times I feel like I am praying for myself for something the Lord is leading me to in the future, or for members of my family. THAT'S ME. That does not mean you will have the same experiences. Why don't you give this a rest for a bit? I believe it would be wise for you to meet with someone face to face and discuss this. If the Holy Spirit is using you as an intercessor in an urgent situation, then He should give you peace over the experience. If you don't have peace, then you need to explore what is going on with someone in person. Perhaps the Pastors if you feel that troubled. You have received a wonderful gift and I know the Lord will open up more to you. Some people have described having an instant powerful experience of praying in tongues for hours or a full day, upon receiving their prayer language. I did not have that experience. Please just don't be frightened. Ask God to help you with your understanding of what is happening to you specifically. Ask Him for revelation knowledge of what is going on. Don't let the devil steal this power from you with Fear. Follow God's leading...this is between you and Him.

OK? Let me know how you are doing now... Norma

HI Rhonda!

You are not a "high" maintenance gal. What Donna described you was the same thing that I was trying to convey. Praying for someone else by the Holy Spirit's choosing. I am very glad that you are having peace about this.

That overwhelming peace is one of the great benefits of praying in the Spirit. Peace and clarity of thought. Amen!

You are having an accelerated experience as compared to my prayer language development. Praise the Lord, you have been seeking after Him so completely that He is responding with awesome experiences.

You are very articulate. I hope you will consider journalizing all these experiences. I believe there will be opportunities for you to use this information to help others as they seek and find this wonderful gift of God. For myself and many other, it is very hard to put into words.

Thank you Rhonda for being so open. I am enjoying getting to know you better. Maybe God will open up opportunities for us to serve together. I would enjoy another lunch or dinner sometime...? See you Sunday.

It has now been about six months since I received the Baptism of the Holy Spirit and my walk with God has grown sweeter and sweeter in that time frame. It is hard, even for me as a writer, to put down in mere words what a difference this has made in my life.

As you will read in the upcoming chapter, receiving the Baptism of the Holy Spirit enabled me to find my primary ministry in the kingdom of God which is intercession. Without tongues, I would not be able to be an effective intercessor and wouldn't be walking in God's perfect will in this area of my life.

Finding my prayer language has brought clarity of thought into my life that wasn't there before. Although I've always been a sharp lady, now my quickness and ability to concentrate is heightened. I also have an amazing compassion for the lost that wasn't there before and a desire to learn and grow in my fellowship with God at higher and deeper levels all the time.

Colors in the world even seem brighter to me. I didn't use to really enjoy music and now music produces such a tremendous reaction inside of me. I've purchased several Christian CD's that I constantly play. Praising and worshipping God through music has taken on a whole new perspective for me since receiving the Baptism of the Holy Spirit.

The Baptism of the Holy Spirit has also brought an enormous ability to overcome sin in my life. Remember me talking about the relationship in my life that almost brought me down? I had tried before to pull away from this relationship to no avail – only to get sucked right back into the situation. Well, after receiving the Baptism of the Holy Spirit, my ability to overcome this sin was greatly heightened… Power over sin in my life was instantly increased – sin just didn't have the pull and weight in my life anymore.

I am a much better mother now than before. My daughter even asked, about a week after I received this gift, about my changed attitude. All my children were immediately aware that Mom had a different attitude –love and joy were overflowing in my heart and this was spilling out into my relationship with my children.

I have also become tender at a level that didn't exist before. I've always been a "rock" – someone who is NOT emotional at all – able to sit through the saddest movie or deal with the most intense events without a single tear in my eye… Since receiving this gift, I am now very tender – music or even hearing scripture will produce a flood of soft tears. I hear stories about hurting or lost people and emotion will fill my chest – I can't stand to think of people not knowing and receiving Christ as their Savior.

I now have an increased boldness and confidence in my walk with God that is unbelievable. God has placed inside of me an undefeatable attitude in regards to things promised in scripture. I know that He that is in me is much greater than he who is in the world – I am fearless with God on my team!

Concluding this chapter brings me to one final thought… Regardless of what denomination you currently belong to I want to encourage you to read through the scripture references listed in this chapter and really pray about what the Bible actually teaches regarding this subject. Then it is my greatest desire that you will begin to earnestly seek this gift. Although it may be helpful to have another person pray with you to receive this gift, it can be (as it was with me) a very personal and private event. In the privacy of your own prayer closet, the Holy Spirit can begin to manifest himself in your prayer time. At that point, He will pray the perfect will of God through your mouth and you will begin operating in a level of sweet and beautiful fellowship with your Lord and Savior. Receiving the Baptism of the Holy Spirit has been the single biggest event – the most life changing event that I have ever experienced - bar none!

Finding my Ministry

As I explained earlier, upon deciding to follow God instead of my flesh with the married gentleman that I worked with, God placed two strong desires in my heart – to learn about tongues and to find my ministry (stop being a Christian liability and start being an asset!) As I thought about this again, I knew that I had accomplished the first thing on God's list and it only took one more day before I found my ministry as well. I guess when God finds a willing heart, He sometimes works double-time to get that person where He needs them to be.

After I had lunch with Pastor Allen, his words about intercessory prayer kept rolling over and over in my head. As I began to sleep that Wednesday night the thoughts about intercession just kept coming and, during the night, I dreamed of praying for others. When I awoke that Thursday morning, I was saying, "I've been chosen" and after a long time in prayer that morning, God spoke to my heart – I now knew that my ministry in the Christian body was intercession! I quickly emailed my two favorite "tongue coaches" to share my news. The following is the email I sent that morning and both their responses later that day:

Good morning ladies,

I had lunch with the Pastors yesterday (like Norma suggested) and Allen was able to help me understand so many things about what is happening to me. He experienced <u>*fear*</u> *a few times in the beginning as well so he reassured me that my reaction to the violent episode the other night was ok and normal...*

Just now after praying again at length, the Holy Spirit spoke to me and showed me my ministry at Cornerstone which was something else Allen and I talked about and even something I think I had talked to you about before (maybe in our last email)...

I don't remember if I told you but almost just as soon as I totally surrendered myself to God over the "Dying to Self" ordeal, I immediately had two things deeply impressed on me - <u>to learn about my prayer language (tongues)</u> and <u>to find my ministry and stop being selfish</u> (start being a Christian asset in other words)...

Now, I believe I've been called to be an intercessor through prayer like Allen described to me. He said that God calls some to be an intercessor and these people may spend hours in prayer each day - that is what is happening to me big time...

Also, when you think about my life circumstances - widowed, working alone at home 80% of the time, commuting an hour each way to church and to a lot of my business meetings, not needing a lot of sleep, and my personality is suited to being alone (I deeply enjoy people but it does not bother me in the least to spend hours by myself) - I have hours and hours alone available to me to pray that most don't have or wouldn't enjoy having...

Yesterday all total and being conservative, I prayed in my prayer language probably close to 4 hours, maybe even more - just the drive both ways yesterday to Tahlequah equaled two - but it doesn't seem like that at all - it's completely effortless - weird deal, huh?

I woke from a dream saying, "I've been chosen" and I just have a smile on my face right now thinking how smart God is - He has given me an awesome ministry just perfectly suited to who I am - a perfect ministry for a Cornerstone commuter with small kids...

Hi Rhonda:

Hallelujah!

I couldn't be happier for you Rhonda! And what a powerful ministry God has given you!!

As I was reading your email I thought and smiled about how God put YOU in the right place and the right people in your life to open up your ministry to you. Every time I hear a story like yours I am in awe of the God we serve. There simply are no words to express His love, compassion and understanding of each individually.

I've gotta go but I look forward to seeing you this weekend.

Hi!

I was thrilled when I read you ate with the pastors and he agreed with the intercession and prayer....I am so proud of you for wanting to get involved in ministry .....you know intercession is a back stage job....very much needed but not a lot of people reward because people don't see you praying.....but a very rewarding spiritual job, when you know your getting things accomplished in the spirit realm.....There's a lady I'll hook you up with who is a friend of mine who is an intercessor and I think you would enjoy talking to her....I don't know if she has email...I'll check....her name is Mary Ann Brown...her husband plays keyboard, and she is working in Tulsa right now.,...but goes to church on Sunday at Cornerstone....

Love ya,

Donna

Ms. Norma

On the Sunday morning following finding my ministry, I was watching for Norma to come into the church. She was always visiting with friends or meeting and greeting visitors so it took me awhile to find her alone so we could talk a little. I had some more questions to ask her and wanted to personally thank her for being so patient with me throughout this whole process.

That day, Norma was later that day than usual to settle into her normal seat. When she did sit down, I quickly scooted over and sat in front of her for a fast chat. I then caught an "eye to eye" gaze with her and <u>I could just see a face full of sadness and exhaustion.</u> It was an intense feeling for me but since finding my prayer language and ministry, I was experiencing new and heightened emotions all the time. We spoke for just a moment and I went back to sit by my daughter for the service.

After arriving home from church and lunch that afternoon, I went for my walk. I hadn't gotten up early enough to walk before we left for church so I took off about 1:30 or so…

I was just praying away in the Spirit as I walked and suddenly, Norma was heavy on my mind. It was just amazing and as I kept praying and walking, this intense emotion about Norma continued…

By the time I arrived home that day, God had laid it on my heart to contact Norma and suggest that I plan a day for her because she needed to relax and unwind – just have some fun. One of the first things that came to mind was making her an appointment for a pedicure and then having a nice lunch with lots of girl talk or something. God was really stirring my heart to reach out to Norma. I could also tell that there might be more to this than just being nice to a new friend – I was thinking that maybe God had a plan for us and we needed some time together to figure out what that was.

Over the course of the next week, Norma and I emailed daily planning for our day. She was taking off work all day on Friday, May 16, 2003 and meeting me in Muskogee for her first pedicure at 9:00 a.m. I had the best time planning for Norma's day of relaxation. I think God knew that I needed to focus attention on someone else besides myself as much as Norma needed a day of relaxation and a good friend in her life.

On that Friday, Norma arrived for her pedicure and I had a cup of flavored coffee and some muffins and cherry bon bons for her to snack on – everyone knows a lady of leisure has to snack on bon bons! After that we had a facial planned for 11:00 and then lunch at a great little Italian restaurant. During lunch, we shared and talked about our past and our dreams. We had an immediate, intense connection with one another. Throughout the balance of the day Norma described to me how she had prayed for a personal intercessor for the past two years and that she thought I was that lady in her life.

I had never heard of a personal intercessor but listening to her that day just took my breath away. You see, Norma had been called into the Ministry a year of so before and was currently in Bible College completing her requirements. She was scheduled to soon graduate from the Practical Ministry Program and was now taking Missions Classes. Norma knew that she was called to have a women's ministry and because of the time requirements and all the public work connected with that job, God had laid it on her heart that she needed a lady in her life whose focus was prayer – specifically praying for her and her ministry.

I left Norma that day about 6:00 with a ditty bag full of goodies for a perfect bubble bath and instructions on how to finish her day to completely "Cure a weary Saint." As I drove home my head was swimming. I believed all Norma had told me and in my Spirit I knew I was the lady she had prayed so hard for during the past two years. It felt like a tremendous responsibility and an awesome opportunity all at the same time. I was so looking forward to developing this friendship and continuing to make myself available for all God had planned for me. Life was beginning to get very interesting.

Meeting Norma has changed my life. Within just a few weeks, so many things in God's plan for my life began to unfold. I had found my prayer language and then my ministry – so funny to me to realize that unless I had received the Baptism of the Holy Spirit and begun to operate in the gift of tongues, I would never have been able to fulfill my role as intercessor – I would not have been able to be fully involved in the primary ministry that God had for my life. Meeting Norma also gave me the opportunity to be involved in the calling on her life as a missionary and her new ministry called Women of Truth Ministries. Realizing my place within this world-wide ministry has been life changing for me in a mighty way.

To conclude this chapter, I am including the actual emails from the day I noticed the emotion in Norma's face and her response to my request to treat her to a day of relaxation. As I was putting this book together and re-reading those emails again – it just amazed me how bold I was that day. I had only eaten with Norma once and had been exchanging email with her for just a week or so. This whole process with Norma was an amazing God-led experience and there is hardly a day that goes by now when I don't thank God for helping me be obedient to his leading that day to reach out to Ms. Norma Rice.

Hey again Norma,

After we returned from lunch and church I went on my walk. I was just walking and praying and then you were really on my mind. I believe the Holy Spirit was prompting me to check on you...

This morning, you looked very tired Norma. You are burning the candle at both ends and you need to remember that working yourself to death, even for the cause of Christ, is not good. You need to take care of yourself and do something relaxing and just for fun – take a breather – get away from all your ministries and just think only about how good God is with your feet propped up and laughing with a new friend...

I'd be glad to arrange for a day-long or a half a day of relaxing for you away from the phone and activity of your busy life. I could pack a wonderful lunch and we could meet at Honor Heights in Muskogee for lunch and enjoy the flowers and birds and lots of girl talk. I also would let you in on one of the best kept secrets in Muskogee – one of my very best friends is a manicurist (semi-retired) that gives 1 hour+ pedicures. I'm not kidding Norma, she massages your leg up to the knee, each toe, soaks, wraps, vibrates, waxes – you name it – she plays soothing Christian music and if you are not careful you would think you were experiencing just a tiny piece of heaven – the appointment with this lady is yours – all you gotta do is say when...

If the park and a professional pedicure don't appeal to you, you could sneak down to my home and (after I take the phone off the hook!), I could give you a Rhonda "special" pedicure – it wouldn't be as good as Diane's but I'm pretty good if I say so myself – We could then each curl up on my big 'ole comfy couch and talk and talk – maybe even crack open a bag of Famous Amos chocolate chip cookies to complete a great day...

Think about it – play hooky for even just a half a day, get that unbelievable pedicure, and let's talk – I think

God wants us to partner in some way - I'm not sure how but I really feel drawn for us to have some time to yak and find out what God's plan is...

Hello Friend:

You know Rhonda I am in complete agreement! I believed that you were the intercessor that I have asked God for. And the email is just a confirmation to me.

There has been a lot going on in my life. I stay very busy, as you know, with ministry and VBI things. But, the stress you saw in my face today was compounded by my daughter's life and my attempts for over 13 years to help her make good decisions. It's a very long story.

Rhonda, when you are in ministry and at the front of groups of people, you have to be very careful about who you share your own trials with. We all have them, but for some reason people don't think you do when God is using you in a leadership role. This is my last week of full time internship at MMI. I am committed to continue to work with the ministry but I can be more flexible with my scheduling. If it would work out for you on Friday I might be able to take the day and combine some "grant" mentoring and finish the day off with a new friend. Man the pedicure sounds pretty great. I have never had a pedicure. Just let me know you thoughts, I know you have a schedule and a life also.

I so appreciate this offer right now. The Lord knows how stubborn I am about crying "uncle." I feel tired and I NEED to be at my best before I leave for the Philippines on June 17th. Thank you for your prayers and your obedience to God's voice!

Wrap-up

I wanted to spend some time at the conclusion of the book driving home the message of God's blessing and provision in my life. I believe the overriding reason that God wants this story on paper is to make people understand that what He has done for me and my family is available to everyone. I want people to be totally convinced that God has been faithful, that His care and provision for my family has been miraculous, and that same thing is available to any and every believer. It is so important for people to understand that God is faithful to do these same kinds of things for all people who are willing to make him the Lord of their life. God desires people who are willing and ready to embrace the Jet Ski mentality – people who are ready to grab God and hold on for an amazing ride through life!

Some people will possibly hear about my life story and only see a life filled with great tragedy but I don't see it that way at all. I see a life where satan has tried very hard to destroy my family and me – where he has attempted to discourage and frustrate me – possibly making me become bitter and angry and destroying my testimony. However, it is one of my greatest desires to let God's love and peace inside of me radiate out to all those with whom I come in contact. I want my life to scream, "Victory through Christ!" I want people to see and understand that a person can allow Christ to walk them through terrible circumstances and restore and bless them in and through the process.

My faith in God and testimony are stronger today than ever before because I have chosen to live every day of my life seeking God and filling myself with all the best He has to offer. I have made a conscious decision to allow my emotions and attitude to be God directed, based upon Truth in God's Word instead of allowing my emotions and attitudes to be guided by circumstances in my life. I believe this has been the key to my overall ability to remain focused and optimistic – firmly believing that God will fulfill the desires of my heart and that He is so good – all the time!

Person after person that have met me and heard of my life story, have been impressed that my children and I are happy and living a blessed life. I try to always be diligent to give God full credit for the place I find myself in life. I could have easily turned to alcohol or pills to fill the void in my heart when my husband passed away and I'm sure that had I followed that avenue my story would be a totally different one. I take no credit at all for surviving my tragedy – I truly believe that walking through the fire and coming out victorious is only possible with God holding your hand and guiding each step that you take!

When thinking of this re-cap, I asked God to show me verses that specifically explain the process of His provision and blessing in my life. Almost everywhere that I look in scripture, I can see evidence of God's tremendous desire to bless and provide for His children, but I knew that there were scriptures that God could use to make maximum impact on each person that reads this story.

In the end, God showed me that there are several primary truths and subsequent scriptures that I need to convey and explain to the reader – primary truths that if applied to any Christian's life will make a "real" difference – a very positive difference in each and every life. These primary truths are:

- Keep God's word on your mind and heart and it will lead you to a stable and prosperous life. James 1:8
- God's favor will surround you like a shield in your life. Psalms 5:12

- God's love for us is an agape love – totally unconditional and always present. Romans 5:8
- God is ONLY and ALWAYS good – God is not the author of confusion or disaster – God is never responsible for evil in our lives. James 1:17
- Fear is not from God – Faith and trust in God brings love, blessing, and a sound mind to us. 2 Timothy 1:7

1) The first verse that immediately comes to mind is Joshua 1:8 (NKJV) - <u>This Book of the Law shall not depart from your mouth, but you shall meditate on it day and night, that you may observe to do according to all that is written in it. For then you will make your way prosperous, and then you will have good success.</u> To me, this scripture is a mighty promise to Christians – by keeping God's word and truth in our heart and operating accordingly, then our way in life will surely be prosperous – we WILL achieve good success. This promise is more than powerful. This

is "real" – God has proven this to me over and over again – it works!

2) I have also spent some time researching the concept of FAVOR in God's eyes and what exactly that means to each and every Christian. I understand favor because I experience it and have for a very long time. Favor means to be pleased with or to be favorable toward something. Favor is also described as pleasure, desire, delight, and to be pleased with. One powerful verse that described this process of favor to me is Psalms 5:12 (NKJV) - For You, O Lord, will bless the righteous; with favor You will surround him as with a shield.

Think about that one – by accepting Jesus Christ as your Savior, you are automatically given all the things of Christ just as He took all your sin (past, present, and future) upon Himself and paid for all of that sin on the cross. Christ became our sin and we then became His righteousness. This beautiful process is known as the doctrine of atonement and assures each Christian that they are the righteousness of God through Christ Jesus. (2 Corinthians 5: 21) At the moment of salvation, we received it ALL – it was a done deal from the beginning... From this point on in our walk with God we just need to align what we are thinking in our head and doing with our bodies to match up with what God has intended for us in our life.

According to this promise in Psalms 5:12, when we allow the righteousness of Christ to manifest itself in our life, the Lord God will bless us and His favor will surround us just like a shield. Of all the situations in my life where I felt and realized I was walking in major favor with God, the story of my house fire is the best example. When my home burned in November 2001, I could dramatically see the favor of God covering my life just like a shield. Instead of that circumstance devastating my family both personally and financially, we were blessed at every turn.

After the fire, we immediately had another place to stay that was fully furnished including the plates in the cabinets, towels in the bathroom, sheets on the bed, and even food in the refrigerator. My homeowner's insurance coverage was more than double the original amount of just a few weeks prior because of God's hand in increasing the amount right before the tragedy. No one in my family even received a single scratch during the fire and as it turns out, almost all our irreplaceable items were salvageable and the items that could easily be replaced were replaced because of adequate insurance.

3) Another thought that God has laid on my heart to convey to the readers of this book is that God is always good and He sometimes protects and blesses us in spite of our lack of fervor in seeking His complete will for our lives. God's love toward us is an agape love. Agape love denotes an undefeatable benevolence and unconquerable goodwill that always seeks the highest good of the other person, no

matter what that person does. It is a self-giving love that spends itself completely on us without requiring anything in return, without considering the worth or the worthlessness - in human terms - of the object of that love. Agape is best described as love "by choice" and it is dependent not on the emotion of the one who loves, but on the will of the one who loves. Agape love perfectly describes the unconditional love God has for the world. He chose to love us.

To illustrate this truth in my life, I need to recap how my story in Christ began. I received Jesus as a young girl who, at the tender age of 6, walked the aisle in a small-town Baptist Church and asked Him to come into her heart. Although I spent my youth attending church, I never really made the decision to give Christ 100% of my life. During the first 19 years of my walk with God, I had assurance of salvation but no intimate fellowship with Him. God, however, was faithful and merciful. He quietly directed me through minefields of bad choices though I wasn't really asking or listening for his guidance or help. I can actually say that I was blessed in spite of myself.

When I think back on this stage in my life, I'm so thankful that God's love and gifts of mercy don't depend on what we are doing or feeling alone... His gifts are given through the goodness of the giver and are not conditional. That point is driven home for me whenever I consider those times in my life that God chose to bless me, even though I was not in sweet fellowship with Him. Romans 5:8 (NKJV) says, "But God demonstrates His own love toward us, in that while we were still sinners, Christ died for us."

Did you catch that? God didn't wait until we were all cleaned up and in perfect fellowship with Him before He sacrificed His only son. He so loved us, with an agape love, that while we were still in our junk, He sent his Son to die on the cross as a sacrifice for our sin - WHILE we were still sinners. He is ALWAYS such a good God!

4) The next point that comes to mind that I want to make sure the readers of my story don't miss is how changing my perception of God in the last couple of years has helped me find peace and contentment in life. Although on the day of my husband's death, I laid on that motel floor in San Diego, California and made Jesus the actual Lord of my life, I did not totally find freedom and peace. I did find a sweeter fellowship, but having the concept in my head that God is the cause of all things in life – good and bad – left me feeling confused... I would search my Bible to try and find answers about "why" God took my husband and my children's father. I went into overdrive trying to be perfect and parent my children perfectly because of a huge fear hanging over me that I would "mess up" and another disaster would soon follow.

During this stage in my Christian growth, I constantly searched scripture and found examples of bad women or bad female attitudes. Because in my mind,

Mike had probably contracted cancer as a result of living a stressful life, my thought was that I had caused him stress and had directly contributed to his death. You see, satan would "twist" those scriptures in my mind and time after time I would rationalize and think that if I had just been a more perfect wife – if I had not caused Mike any kind of stress at all then he would not have died.

When I started attending church at Cornerstone and realized that so many of my own thoughts were being filtered through a Calvinistic viewpoint that directly conflicted with scripture, many things about God began to make more sense to me. I was able to really begin to see God as my Father – as a tender Father that wanted only blessing and good things for my life. I began to see God as my protector and champion – not someone up in the clouds waiting for me to "screw up" so he could zap me with one disaster after another. In James 1:17 (NKJV) we have the promise that – Every good gift and every perfect gift is from above, and comes down from the Father of Lights, with whom there is no variation or shadow of turning. There could not be a more clear verse to illustrate the fact that only good and perfect things come from God – there's never any variation to that theme – ever!

Now I totally understand that many times, because of sin and disobedience, we bring unpleasant consequences upon ourselves. However, realizing that God is the author of ONLY GOOD things made a huge impact upon my fellowship with him. With this new perception of God it quickly became a joy to serve God!

(5) In the NKJV Bible, 2 Timothy 1:7 says –For God has not given us a spirit of fear, but of power and of love and of a sound mind. WOW! Now this is a verse for a widowed mom with 4 children. As trial after trial has come into my path, I am comforted by these words. Fear does not come from God – Fear is evil and should be resisted and not allowed to manifest itself in our lives. God gave us a

spirit of love and an ability to have a sound mind even in the midst of difficult circumstances.

Now I could sit here and write one truth and scripture after another and show through my own life examples how God fulfilled his promises to me and my family time and time again. However, there has to come a point where one story ends and another begins.

So, I'm sitting here tonight smiling as I come to the conclusion of this first book – mostly thinking about how exciting it will be to prepare the sequel to Jet Skiing with God, now titled: Skydiving with the Almighty! (The adventure intensifies!) Since joining a Charismatic church and opening myself up to God's full truth, I have grown so much in my spiritual maturity and have also found MANY pleasant surprises that I would have never expected. Skydiving with the Almighty (The adventure intensified!) will be my continuing story – my amazing journey through understanding fellowship with God at an even more powerful and anointed level and how that fellowship has opened new and exciting doors of ministry for me all over the world. All in all, I think book #2 will be more powerful and life changing for people than this first one...

Concluding this book brings closure to this section of my life story. God wanted this story on paper and I've been obedient. I just hope and pray that through reading what God has done in my life you will be inspired to go for it – work on opening yourself up for all God has for you – you will never, ever regret that decision!

About The Author

Rhonda Clemons lives in Northeastern, Oklahoma with her four beautiful children – Tyler (21), Emily (15), Mason (8), and Noah (6) where she owns and operates her own consulting and grant writing business. She is also active serving as the vice-president of Women of Truth Ministries, Inc. whose founding mission is to empower women with the truth of who they are and God's plan for their life. Through her role in WTM, she travels the U.S. and abroad telling her story of personal victory through Jesus Christ over a series of overwhelming personal tragedies. Rhonda leads a very full life keeping up with four active children and also serving faithfully in her home church – Cornerstone Fellowship in Tahlequah, OK.

Printed in the United States
21402LVS00001B/64-111